STANDARD GRADE | GENERAL

MATHEMATICS
2008-2012

 SQA

 BrightRED
PUBLISHING

© Scottish Qualifications Authority
All rights reserved. Copying prohibited. No part of this publication may be reproduced, stored in a retrieval system, or transmitted in any form or by any means, electronic, mechanical, photocopying, recording or otherwise.

First exam published in 2008.
Published by Bright Red Publishing Ltd, 6 Stafford Street, Edinburgh EH3 7AU
tel: 0131 220 5804 fax: 0131 220 6710 info@brightredpublishing.co.uk www.brightredpublishing.co.uk

ISBN 978-1-84948-253-0

A CIP Catalogue record for this book is available from the British Library.

Bright Red Publishing is grateful to the copyright holders, as credited on the final page of the Question Section, for permission to use their material. Every effort has been made to trace the copyright holders and to obtain their permission for the use of copyright material. Bright Red Publishing will be happy to receive information allowing us to rectify any error or omission in future editions.

STANDARD GRADE | GENERAL

2008

[BLANK PAGE]

FOR OFFICIAL USE

G

	KU	RE
Total marks		

2500/403

NATIONAL
QUALIFICATIONS
2008

THURSDAY, 8 MAY
10.40 AM – 11.15 AM

MATHEMATICS
STANDARD GRADE
General Level
Paper 1
Non-calculator

Fill in these boxes and read what is printed below.

Full name of centre

Town

Forename(s)

Surname

Date of birth

Day   Month   Year   Scottish candidate number   Number of seat

1 **You may not use a calculator.**

2 Answer as many questions as you can.

3 Write your working and answers in the spaces provided. Additional space is provided at the end of this question-answer book for use if required. If you use this space, write clearly the number of the question involved.

4 Full credit will be given only where the solution contains appropriate working.

5 Before leaving the examination room you must give this book to the invigilator. If you do not you may lose all the marks for this paper.

LI 2500/403 6/61470

FORMULAE LIST

Circumference of a circle: $C = \pi d$

Area of a circle: $A = \pi r^2$

Curved surface area of a cylinder: $A = 2\pi rh$

Volume of a cylinder: $V = \pi r^2 h$

Volume of a triangular prism: $V = Ah$

Theorem of Pythagoras:

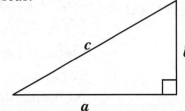

$$a^2 + b^2 = c^2$$

Trigonometric ratios
in a right angled
triangle:

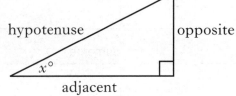

$$\tan x° = \frac{\textbf{opposite}}{\textbf{adjacent}}$$

$$\sin x° = \frac{\textbf{opposite}}{\textbf{hypotenuse}}$$

$$\cos x° = \frac{\textbf{adjacent}}{\textbf{hypotenuse}}$$

Gradient:

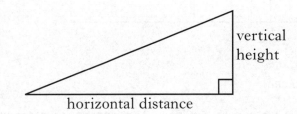

$$\textbf{Gradient} = \frac{\textbf{vertical height}}{\textbf{horizontal distance}}$$

Marks | KU | RE

1. Carry out the following calculations.

(a) $12 \cdot 76 - 3 \cdot 18 + 4 \cdot 59$

$$\begin{array}{r} {}^0 12 \cdot {}^6 \not{7} 6 \\ -03 \cdot 18 \\ \hline 9 \cdot 58 \end{array}$$

$$\begin{array}{r} 9 \cdot 58 \\ +4 \cdot 59 \\ \hline 14 \cdot 17 \end{array}$$

$\boxed{14 \cdot 17}$

1

(b) $6 \cdot 39 \times 9$

$$\begin{array}{r} 6 \cdot 39 \\ \times 9 \\ \hline 57 \cdot 51 \end{array}$$

1

(c) $8 \cdot 74 \div 200$

$$\begin{array}{r} 4 \cdot 37 \\ 2 \overline{) 8 \cdot 7^1 4} \end{array}$$

$0 \cdot 0437$

1

(d) $\frac{5}{6}$ of 420

$$\begin{array}{r} 070 \\ 6 \overline{) 420} \end{array}$$

$$\begin{array}{r} 70 \\ \times 5 \\ \hline 350 \end{array}$$

2

[Turn over

Marks   KU   RE

2. In the "Fame Show", the percentage of telephone votes cast for each act is shown below.

Plastik Money	23%
Brian Martins	35%
Starshine	30%
Carrie Gordon	12%

Altogether 15 000 000 votes were cast.

How many votes did Starshine receive?

1⊙ 15000000

1500000
× 3
4 500000

3

Marks | KU | RE

3. AB and BC are two sides of a kite ABCD.

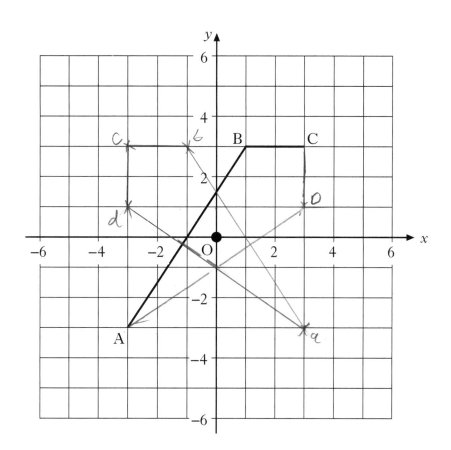

(*a*) Plot point D to complete kite ABCD.   **1**

(*b*) Reflect kite ABCD in the **y-axis**.

3

Marks | KU | RE

4. Europe is the world's second smallest continent.

Its area is approximately 10 400 000 square kilometres.

Write this number in scientific notation.

$10 \, 400 \, 000 \, km^2$

7×10^2

1.04×10^7

5000

$= 5.0 \times 10^3$

2

Marks | KU | RE

5. Samantha is playing the computer game "Castle Challenge".

To enter the castle she needs the correct four digit code.

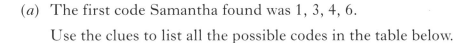

The computer gives her some clues:

- only digits 1 to 9 can be used
- each digit is greater than the one before
- the sum of all four digits is 14.

(*a*) The first code Samantha found was 1, 3, 4, 6.

Use the clues to list all the possible codes in the table below.

1	3	4	6
1	2	5	6
1	2	3	8
1	2	4	7
2	3	4	5

12357

3

(*b*) The computer gives Samantha another clue.

- three of the digits in the code are prime numbers

What is the four digit code Samantha needs to enter the castle?

1 2 3 8

1

[Turn over

Marks | KU | RE

6.

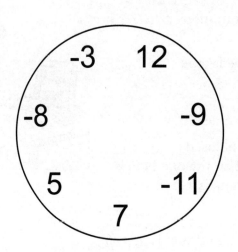

The circle above contains seven numbers.

Find the three numbers from the circle which add up to −10.

You must show your working.

$7, -8, -9$

$12 - 9 - 3$

$-10 + 12 = 2$

$-10 + 5 = -5$

$-10 + 7 = -3$

3

Marks | KU | RE

7. The cost of sending a letter depends on the size of the letter and the weight of the letter.

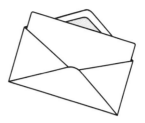

Format	Weight	Cost	
		1st Class Mail	**2nd Class Mail**
Letter	0–100 g	34p	24p
Large Letter	0–100 g	48p	40p
	101–250 g	70p	60p
	251–500 g	98p	83p
	501–750 g	142p	120p

Claire sends a letter weighing 50 g by 2nd class mail.

She also sends a large letter weighing 375 g by 1st class mail.

Use the table above to calculate the total cost.

£00.24
+ £00.98
————
£01.22

3

[**Turn over**

Marks KU RE

8. Four girls and two boys decide to organise a tennis tournament for themselves.

Each name is written on a plastic token and put in a bag.

(*a*) What is the probability that the first token drawn from the bag has a girl's name on it?

4 : 2

1

(*b*) The first token drawn from the bag has a girl's name on it.

This token is **not** returned to the bag.

What is the probability that the next token drawn from the bag has a boy's name on it?

2 : 3

2

DO NOT WRITE IN THIS MARGIN

Marks | KU | RE

9.

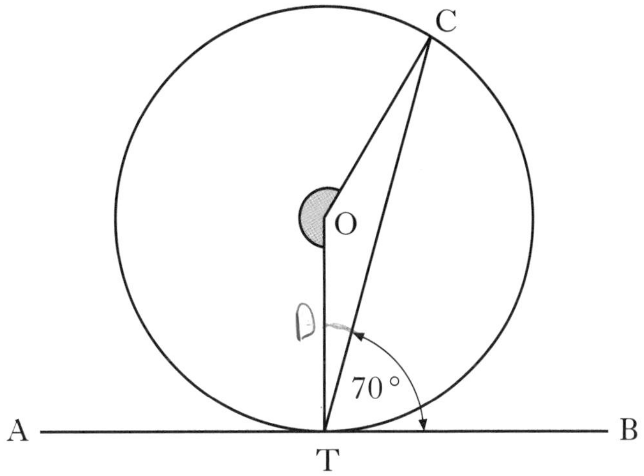

D-20°

In the diagram above:

- O is the centre of the circle
- AB is a tangent to the circle at T
- angle BTC = 70 °.

Calculate the size of the shaded angle TOC.

220°

3

[*END OF QUESTION PAPER*]

ADDITIONAL SPACE FOR ANSWERS

KU   RE

Total
marks

G

2500/404

NATIONAL
QUALIFICATIONS
2008

THURSDAY, 8 MAY
11.35 AM – 12.30 PM

MATHEMATICS
STANDARD GRADE
General Level
Paper 2

Fill in these boxes and read what is printed below.

Full name of centre

Town

Forename(s)

Surname

Date of birth

Day Month Year   Scottish candidate number   Number of seat

1 **You may use a calculator.**

2 Answer as many questions as you can.

3 Write your working and answers in the spaces provided. Additional space is provided at the end of this question-answer book for use if required. If you use this space, write clearly the number of the question involved.

4 Full credit will be given only where the solution contains appropriate working.

5 Before leaving the examination room you must give this book to the invigilator. If you do not you may lose all the marks for this paper.

FORMULAE LIST

Circumference of a circle: $C = \pi d$

Area of a circle: $A = \pi r^2$

Curved surface area of a cylinder: $A = 2\pi rh$

Volume of a cylinder: $V = \pi r^2 h$

Volume of a triangular prism: $V = Ah$

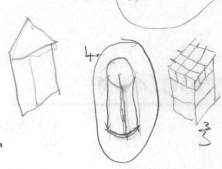

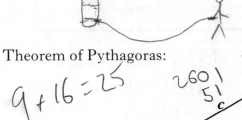

Theorem of Pythagoras:

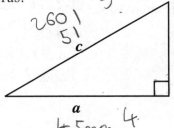

$$a^2 + b^2 = c^2$$

Trigonometric ratios in a right angled triangle:

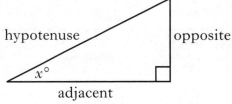

hypotenuse   opposite

$x°$

adjacent

$$\tan x° = \frac{\text{opposite}}{\text{adjacent}}$$

$$\sin x° = \frac{\text{opposite}}{\text{hypotenuse}}$$

$$\cos x° = \frac{\text{adjacent}}{\text{hypotenuse}}$$

Gradient:

vertical height

horizontal distance

$$\text{Gradient} = \frac{\text{vertical height}}{\text{horizontal distance}}$$

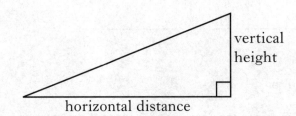

Marks | KU | RE

1. Corrina has a part time job in a local pottery.

She paints designs on coffee mugs.

Her basic rate of pay is £6·25 per hour.

She also gets paid an extra 22 pence for every mug she paints.

Last week Corrina worked 15 hours and painted 40 mugs.

How much was she paid?

£6.25
X 15
£31.25
62.50
93.75

00.22
X 40
00
8.80

£93.75 + £8.80

£102.55

3

[Turn over

Marks | KU | R|

2. Charlie's new car has an on-board computer.

At the end of a journey the car's computer displays the information below.

Journey information

distance **157.5 miles**

average speed **45 miles/hour**

Use the information above to calculate the time he has taken for his journey.

Give your answer in hours and minutes.

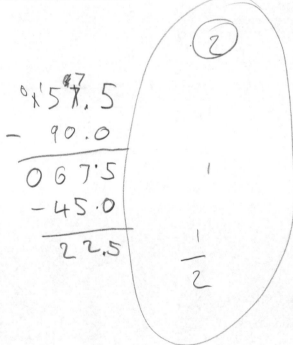

$$157.5$$
$$-\ 90.0$$
$$\overline{\ \ 067.5}$$
$$-45.0$$
$$\overline{\ \ 22.5}$$

1

$\dfrac{1}{2}$

3hrs 30mins

4

Marks | KU | RE

3.

Ben needs 550 grams of flour to bake two small loaves of bread.

(a) How many **kilograms** of flour will he need for thirteen small loaves?

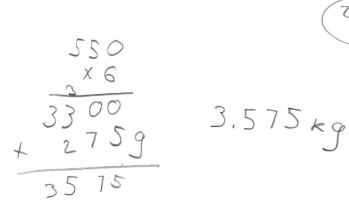

$\boxed{275g}$

$$550$$
$$\times 6$$
$$\overline{3300}$$
$$+ 275g$$
$$\overline{3575}$$

$3.575 \, kg$

2

Ben buys his flour in 1·5 kilogram bags.

(b) How many bags of flour will he need to bake the thirteen small loaves?

3

1

[Turn over

Marks KU RI

4. Mhairi makes necklaces in M-shapes using silver bars.

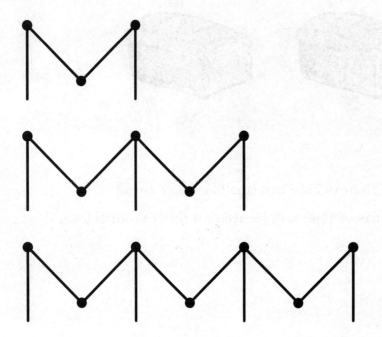

(a) Complete the table below.

Number of M-shapes (m)	1	2	3	4		15
Number of bars (b)	4	7	10	13		46

2

(b) Write down a formula for calculating the number of bars (b) when you know the number of M-shapes (m).

$$b = (M \times 3) + 1$$

2

(c) Mhairi has 76 silver bars.

How many M-shapes can she make?

$$76 = (M \times 3) + 1$$

$$M = 75 \div 3$$

$$76 - 1 = (m \times 3)$$
$$75 = (m \times 3)$$

2

Marks | KU | RE

5. Lewis is designing a bird box for his garden.

The dimensions for the side of the box are shown in the diagram below.

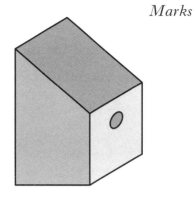

26 cm

18 cm

15 cm

Calculate the length of side PS.

Do not use a scale drawing.

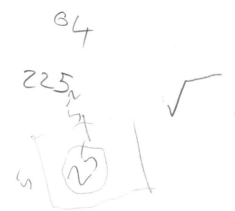

$$\sqrt{289} = 17$$

4

[Turn over

Marks | KU | RE

6. Gordon buys an antique teapot for £95.

   He sells it on an Internet auction site for £133.

   Calculate his percentage profit.

$$133 - 95 = 38 \qquad \frac{38}{95} \times \frac{100}{1} \qquad 40\%$$

$$\frac{10}{40} \times \frac{100}{1}$$

3

7. A piece of glass from a stained glass window is shown below.

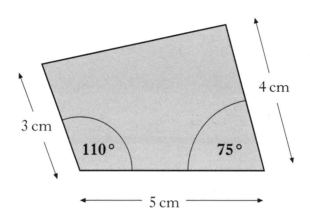

A larger piece of glass, the same shape, is to be made using a scale of 2:1.

Make an accurate drawing of the larger piece of glass.

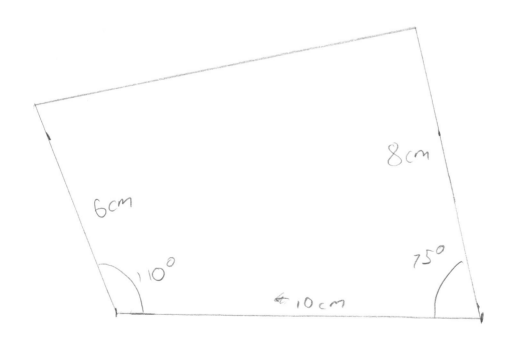

3

[Turn over

DO NOT WRITE IN THIS MARGIN

Marks	KU	RE

8. (*a*) Solve algebraically

$$7t - 3 = t + 45.$$

7t = t + 45 - 3

-t
7t = +42

t = 7

6t = 42
t = 42 ÷ 6

3

(*b*) Factorise fully

$$20x - 12y.$$ = 200

4(5x - 3y) = 200

2

Marks

KU	RE

9. Ian is making a sign for Capaldi's Ice Cream Parlour.

The sign will have two equal straight edges and a semi-circular edge.

Each straight edge is 2·25 metres long and the radius of the semi-circle is 0·9 metres.

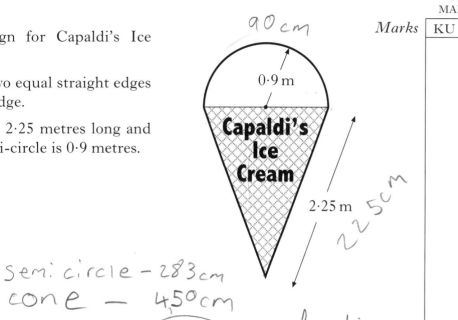

90 cm

0·9 m

2·25 m

225cm

Calculate the perimeter of the sign.

Semi circle - 283cm
cone - 450cm

7.33m

d - diameter

$C = \pi d \div 2$

4

[Turn over

DO NOT WRITE IN THIS MARGIN

Marks KU RE

10. Natalie wanted to know the average number of hours cars were parked in a car park.

She did a survey of 100 cars which were parked in the car park on a particular day.

Her results are shown below.

Parking time (hours)	*Frequency*	*Parking time* × *frequency*
1	28	28
2	22	44
3	10	30
4	15	60
5	11	55
6	5	30
7	9	63
	Total = 100	Total = 310

Complete the above table and find the mean parking time per car.

3.1 hrs

3

Marks | KU | RE

11. Circular tops for yoghurt cartons are cut from a strip of metal foil as shown below.

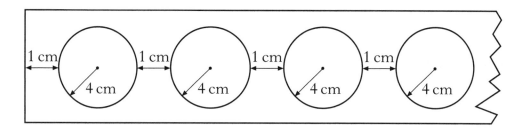

The radius of each top is 4 centimetres.

The gap between each top is 1 centimetre.

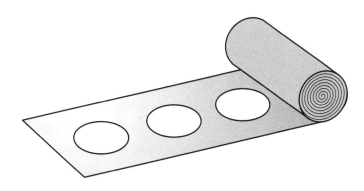

How many tops can be cut from a strip of foil 7 metres long?

77

4

Marks | KU | RE

12. A boat elevator is used to take a boat from the lower canal to the upper canal.

The boat elevator is in the shape of a triangle.

The length of the hypotenuse is 109 metres.

The height of the triangle is 45 metres.

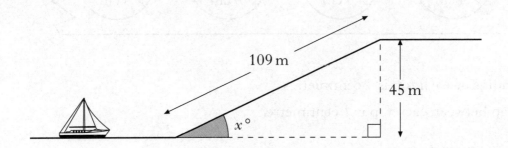

Calculate the size of the shaded angle $x°$.

$$\sin x° = \frac{\text{opposite } 45m}{\text{hypotenuse } 109m}$$

$$x = 24°$$

3

13. A wheelie bin is in the shape of a cuboid.

The dimensions of the bin are:

- length 70 centimetres
- breadth 60 centimetres
- height 95 centimetres.

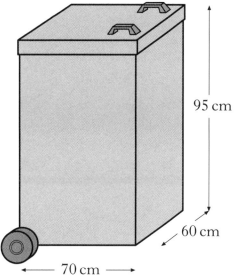

95 cm

60 cm

70 cm

(a) Calculate the volume of the bin.

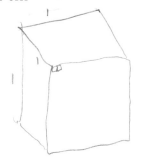

$$L \times b \times h = 399000 \text{ cm}^3$$

$$0.399 \text{ m}^3$$

2

(b) The council is considering a new design of wheelie bin.

The new bin will have the same volume as the old one.

The base of the new bin is to be a square of side 55 centimetres.

Calculate the height of the new wheelie bin.

3025 cm2

$$(l \times b) \times h = 399000 \text{ cm}^3$$
$$3025 \times h = 399000$$
$$h = \frac{399000}{3025} = 132 \text{ cm}$$

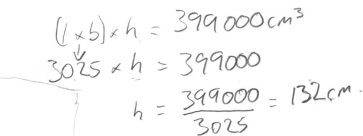
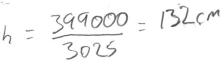
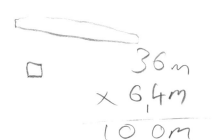

36 m
× 6,4 m
100 m

3

[END OF QUESTION PAPER]

ADDITIONAL SPACE FOR ANSWERS

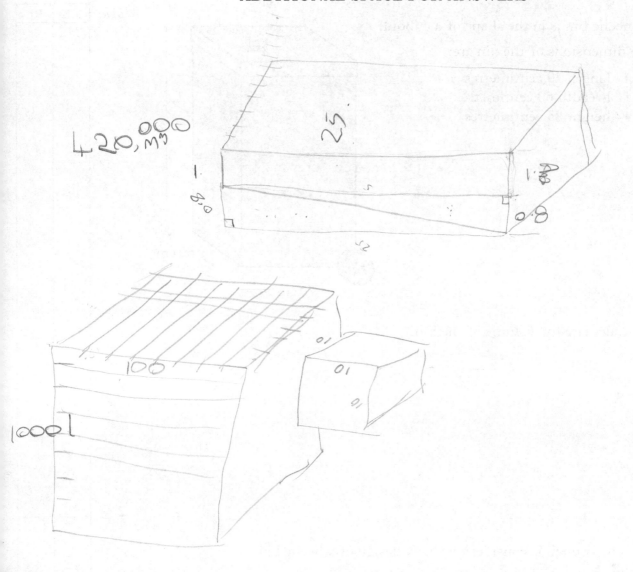

[BLANK PAGE]

FOR OFFICIAL USE

G

	KU	RE
Total marks		

2500/403

NATIONAL
QUALIFICATIONS
2009

WEDNESDAY, 6 MAY
10.40 AM – 11.15 AM

MATHEMATICS
STANDARD GRADE
General Level
Paper 1
Non-calculator

Fill in these boxes and read what is printed below.

Full name of centre

Town

Forename(s)

Surname

Date of birth

Day　Month　Year　　Scottish candidate number　　Number of seat

1　**You may not use a calculator.**

2　Answer as many questions as you can.

3　Write your working and answers in the spaces provided. Additional space is provided at the end of this question-answer book for use if required. If you use this space, write clearly the number of the question involved.

4　Full credit will be given only where the solution contains appropriate working.

5　Before leaving the examination room you must give this book to the invigilator. If you do not you may lose all the marks for this paper.

FORMULAE LIST

Circumference of a circle: $C = \pi d$

Area of a circle: $A = \pi r^2$

Curved surface area of a cylinder: $A = 2\pi rh$

Volume of a cylinder: $V = \pi r^2 h$

Volume of a triangular prism: $V = Ah$

Theorem of Pythagoras:

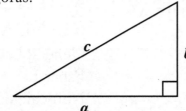

$$a^2 + b^2 = c^2$$

Trigonometric ratios
in a right angled
triangle:

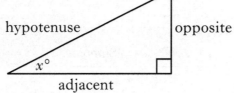

$$\tan x° = \frac{\text{opposite}}{\text{adjacent}}$$

$$\sin x° = \frac{\text{opposite}}{\text{hypotenuse}}$$

$$\cos x° = \frac{\text{adjacent}}{\text{hypotenuse}}$$

Gradient:

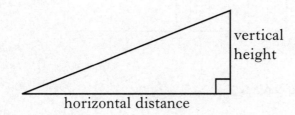

$$\textbf{Gradient} = \frac{\textbf{vertical height}}{\textbf{horizontal distance}}$$

Marks | KU | RE

1. Carry out the following calculations.

(a) $17 \cdot 3 - 14 \cdot 86$

$$17.\overset{6}{3}\overset{2}{0}$$
$$-14.86$$
$$\overline{02 \cdot 44}$$

1

(b) 23×6000

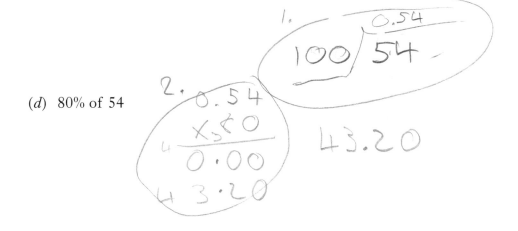

$$234$$
$$\times 6$$
$$\overline{1380} = 138'000$$
$$\times 1000$$

1

(c) $256 \cdot 9 \div 7$

$$1. \quad 100 \overline{\smash{\big)}54} \quad \frac{0.54}{}$$

1

(d) 80% of 54

$$2. \quad \frac{0.54}{\times 80}$$
$$\overline{0 \cdot 00}$$
$$43 \cdot 20$$

$$43.20$$

2

[Turn over

for 1. move numbers two
spaces to the right of
the decimal point (·).

Marks KU RI

2. An old unit of measurement called a fluid ounce is equal to 0·0296 litres.

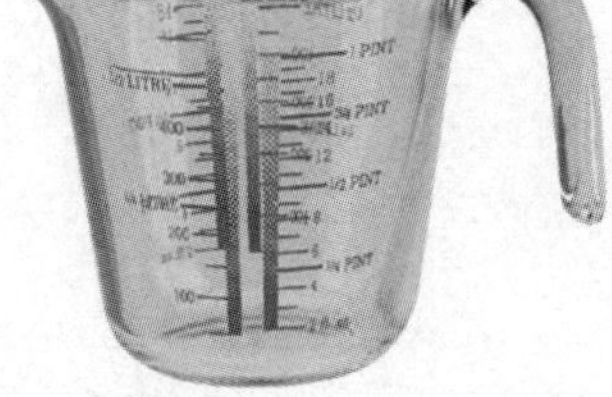

Write 0·0296 in scientific notation.

2.96×10^{-2}

2

Marks   KU   RE

3. Samira is designing a chain belt.

Each section of the belt is made from metal rings as shown below.

 **1 section, 4 rings**

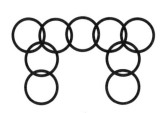 **2 sections, 9 rings**

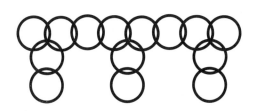 **3 sections**

(*a*) Complete the table below.

$$5\overline{)878} \quad \frac{15 \ r3}{}$$

Number of sections (*s*)	1	2	3	4	5		11
Number of metal rings (*r*)	4	9	14	19	24		

2

(*b*) Write down a formula for calculating the number of rings (*r*), when you know the number of sections (*s*).

$$r = (4s + s) - 1$$

$$r = (4 \times 1) + (11 - 1)$$
$$r = 44 + 10$$
$$r = 54$$

2

(*c*) Samira uses 79 rings to make her belt.

How many sections does her belt have?

$$r = 55 - 1$$
$$79 = 55 - 1$$
$$80 = 55$$

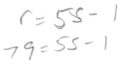

$$79 = (4 \times s) + (s - 1)$$
$$79 - (s - 1) = (4 \times s)$$
$$78 - s = (4 \times s)$$

(16)

$$78 = (4 \times s) + s$$
$$78 = 5s$$
$$\frac{78}{5} =$$

2

4. A floor is to be tiled using tiles shaped like this.

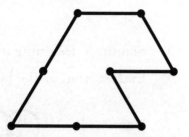

Here is part of the tiling.

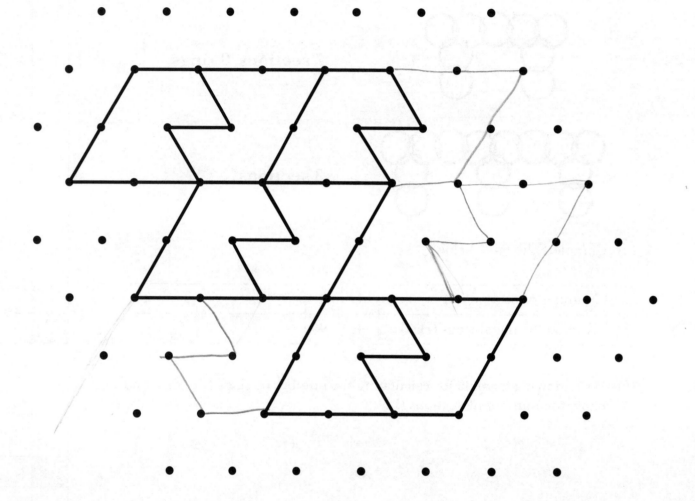

Draw **four** more tiles to continue the tiling.

3

Marks | KU | RE

5. (a) On the grid below, plot the points A(2, 6), B(8, 2) and C(6, –1).

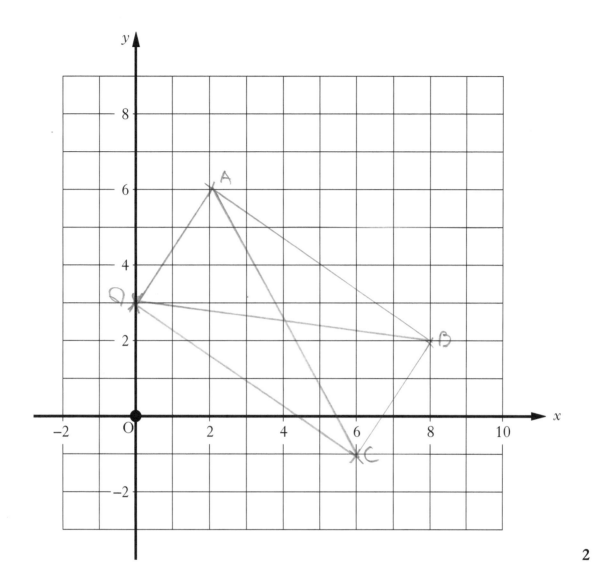

2

(b) Plot a fourth point D so that ABCD is a rectangle.   1

(c) On the grid, show the point where the diagonals of the rectangle intersect.

Write down the coordinates of this point.

$(4, 2.5)$

2

Marks   KU   RE

6. In July the average temperature in Anchorage, Alaska is 9 °C.

By January the average temperature has fallen by 26 °C.

What is the average temperature in Anchorage in January?

$-17 °C$

2

Marks | KU | RE

7. Joe is making a fruit pudding on Scottish Master Chef.

In the fruit pudding recipe the ratio of raspberries to blackberries is 5:1.

Joe's fruit pudding must contain a **total** of 240 grams of fruit.

Calculate the weight of raspberries in his pudding.

40 200g

3

[Turn over

Marks

8. Each pupil in a science class is growing a plant.

A few weeks later the height of each plant is measured.

The heights in centimetres are shown below.

6·3   5·4   5·8   7·0   6·2   7·6   8·3   8·4   5·3   8·8

8·5   5·6   6·8   6·5   6·1   6·7   7·4   7·6   5·3

(*a*) Display these results in an ordered stem and leaf diagram.

```
5 | 3 3 4 6 8
6 | 1 2 3 5 7 8
7 | 0 4 6 6
8 | 3 4 5 8
```

3

(*b*) Find the median height.

6.7

1

Marks   KU   RE

9. In the diagram below:

• triangle ABD is isosceles with AB = AD
• angle DAB = 34°
• angle ABC = 90°
• angle BCD = 20°.

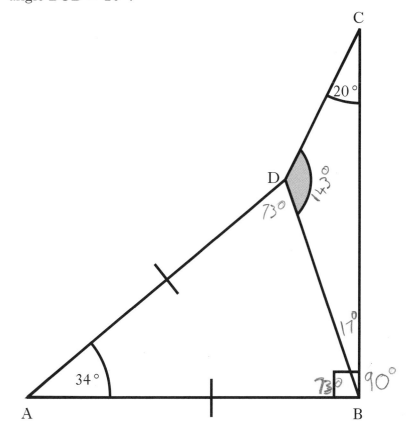

Calculate the size of the shaded angle BDC.

143°

3

[END OF QUESTION PAPER]

ADDITIONAL SPACE FOR ANSWERS

FOR OFFICIAL USE

KU   RE

Total marks

2500/404

NATIONAL
QUALIFICATIONS
2009

WEDNESDAY, 6 MAY
11.35 AM – 12.30 PM

MATHEMATICS
STANDARD GRADE
General Level
Paper 2

G

Fill in these boxes and read what is printed below.

Full name of centre

Town

Forename(s)

Surname

Date of birth

Day Month Year   Scottish candidate number   Number of seat

1 **You may use a calculator.**

2 Answer as many questions as you can.

3 Write your working and answers in the spaces provided. Additional space is provided at the end of this question-answer book for use if required. If you use this space, write clearly the number of the question involved.

4 Full credit will be given only where the solution contains appropriate working.

5 Before leaving the examination room you must give this book to the invigilator. If you do not you may lose all the marks for this paper.

FORMULAE LIST

Circumference of a circle: $C = \pi d$

Area of a circle: $A = \pi r^2$

Curved surface area of a cylinder: $A = 2\pi rh$

Volume of a cylinder: $V = \pi r^2 h$

Volume of a triangular prism: $V = Ah$

Theorem of Pythagoras:

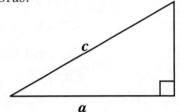

$$a^2 + b^2 = c^2$$

Trigonometric ratios
in a right angled
triangle:

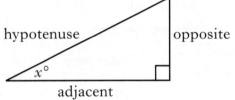

$\tan x° = \dfrac{\text{opposite}}{\text{adjacent}}$

$\sin x° = \dfrac{\text{opposite}}{\text{hypotenuse}}$

$\cos x° = \dfrac{\text{adjacent}}{\text{hypotenuse}}$

Gradient:

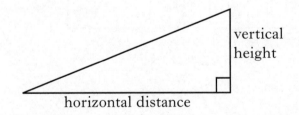

$\textbf{Gradient} = \dfrac{\textbf{vertical height}}{\textbf{horizontal distance}}$

DO NOT WRITE IN THIS MARGIN

Marks | KU | RE

1. Naveen drives from Dumfries to Manchester.

A 28 mile part of his journey is affected by roadworks.

It takes him 40 minutes to drive this part of his journey.

Calculate his average speed for this part of his journey.

Give your answer in miles per hour.

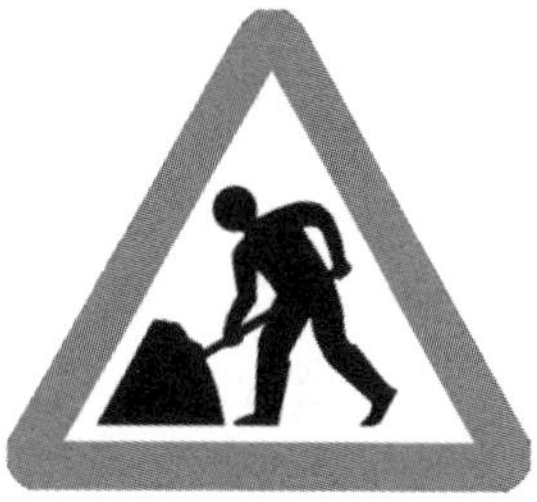

42 mph

3

[Turn over

Marks   KU   R

2. Helen travels between Glasgow and Edinburgh by train.

She buys a monthly TravelPass which costs £264·30.

A daily return ticket would cost £16·90.

Last month Helen made 19 return journeys.

How much did she save by buying the TravelPass?

16.90
× 19
£152·10
169·00
£321·10

£321·10
−£264·30
056·80

£56.80

264·30
+ 56·80
321·10

3

Marks | KU | RE

3. A semi-circular window in the school assembly hall is made from three identical panes of glass.

During a recent storm one pane of glass was damaged.

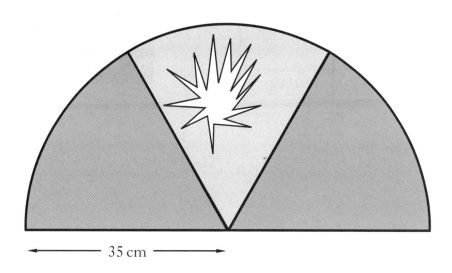

←———— 35 cm ————→

The semi-circle has a radius of 35 centimetres.

Calculate the area of the damaged pane of glass.

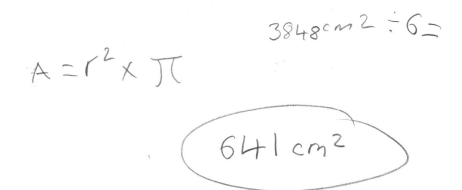

$3848 cm^2 \div 6 =$

$A = r^2 \times \pi$

$641 cm^2$

3

[Turn over

Marks | KU | RI

4. John is going to see a movie.

The movie has an evening and a late night showing.

	Evening showing	Late night showing
Start time	17:50	
Finish time	20:05	01:10

(*a*) How long does the movie last?

2: 15

1

(*b*) When does the late night showing start?

10:55

2

Marks KU | RE

5. (*a*) Factorise

$$6c - 15d.$$

$$3(2c - 5d)$$

(*b*) Simplify

$$5(a + 1) + 2(5 - 2a).$$

$$5a + 5 + 10 - 4a$$

$$5a + 15 - 4a$$

$$a + 15$$

2

3

[Turn over

Marks | KU | RE

6. David is trying to decide which channel mixes to buy for his TV system.

The cost of each is:

- Drama Mix   £7
- Sport Mix   £20
- Movies Mix   £15
- Kids Mix   £12
- Music Mix   £10

He has decided to buy four different mixes.

One possible selection and its cost are shown in the table below.

(a) Complete the table showing all the possible selections and the cost of each.

Selections				Cost
Drama	Sport	Movies	Music	£52
Sport	movies	kids	music	£57
movies	kids	music	Drama	£44
kids	music	Drama	sport	£49
KIDS	Drama	Sport	movies	54

3

(b) David can spend up to £55 for his selection.

Which selection can he **not** buy?

Sport, movies, kids, music

1

(handwritten margin notes: 64; 2 KIDS; 7 DRAMA; 20 SPORT; 15 MOVIES; 10 MUSIC)

DO NOT WRITE IN THIS MARGIN

Marks | KU | RE

7. Last week Theresa asked 76 students to record how many hours they spent doing homework.

The results are shown below.

Homework hours	*Frequency*	*Homework hours* × *frequency*
1	16	16
2	12	24
3	18	54
4	11	44
5	8	40
6	6	36
7	5	35
	Total = 76	Total = 249

Complete the above table and find the **mean** time spent on homework last week.

Round your answer to 1 decimal place.

3.3

4

Marks | KU | RE

8. A steel plate in the shape of an isosceles triangle is used to strengthen a bridge.

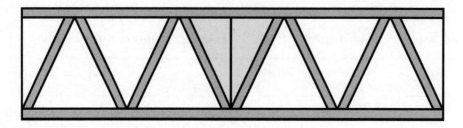

The dimensions of the isosceles triangle are shown below.

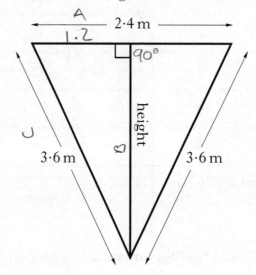

Calculate the height of the steel plate.

Do not use a scale drawing.

$$A^2 + B^2 = C^2$$

$$1.44 + B^2 = 12.96$$

$$B^2 = 12.96 - 1.44$$

$$\sqrt{11.52} = 3.4\,m$$

4

Marks | KU | RE

9.

Pizza Perfection — free delivery				
	Deep Base		Thin Base	
	9-inch	12-inch	9-inch	12-inch
Margherita	£3·60	£5·00	£3·30	£4·60
Mushroom	£4·25	£5·80	£4·15	£5·50
Pepperoni	£5·00	£6·30	£4·90	£6·00
Vegetarian	£5·05	£6·35	£4·95	£6·05
Hot Spicy	£5·15	£6·45	£5·05	£6·15

Iona and her friends order some pizzas to be delivered.

They order a 9-inch Hot Spicy deep base, a 12-inch Margherita deep base and two 12-inch Vegetarian thin base.

Find the total cost of the order.

£5.15
£5.00
£6.05
+ £6.05
———
£22.25

3

[Turn over

Marks | KU | RE

10. Susan has £6200 in her Clydeside Bank account.

Clydeside Bank pays interest at 2·5% per annum.

Highland Bank pays interest at 3·7% per annum.

How much more money would Susan get in interest if she moved her £6200 to the Highland Bank for one year?

$$£6200 \times 2.5 \div 100 = £155.00$$

$$£6200 \times 3.7 \div 100 = £229.40$$

$$£229.40$$
$$- £155.00$$
$$\overline{}$$
$$£74.40$$

3

Marks | KU | RE

11. The shaded part of a garden light is triangular.

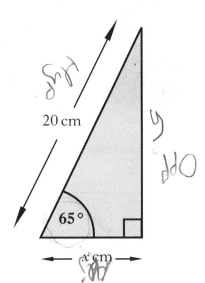

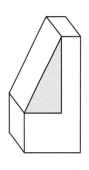

- the triangle is right angled
- the sloping edge is 20 centimetres long
- the angle between the base and the sloping edge is 65°.

Calculate the value of x.

$$\sin x = \frac{opposite}{hypotenuse}$$

$$\sin 25_{cm} = \frac{x}{20}$$

$$0.42 = \frac{x}{20}$$

$$20 \times 0.42 = x$$

$$x = 8.4$$

3

Marks   KU   RE

12. The local council is installing a new children's playpark using a rubberised material.

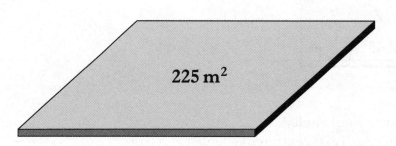

225 m²

The area of the rectangular playpark is 225 square metres.

The new playpark must have a depth of 12 centimetres.

The council has ordered 30 cubic metres of the rubberised material for the playpark.

Will this be enough?

Give a reason for your answer.

yes because 225 × 0.12 = 27

3

Marks

KU	RE

13. An off shore wind farm is on a bearing of 115° and at a distance of 90 kilometres from Eyemouth.

Using a scale of 1 centimetre to represent 10 kilometres, show the position of the wind farm on the diagram below.

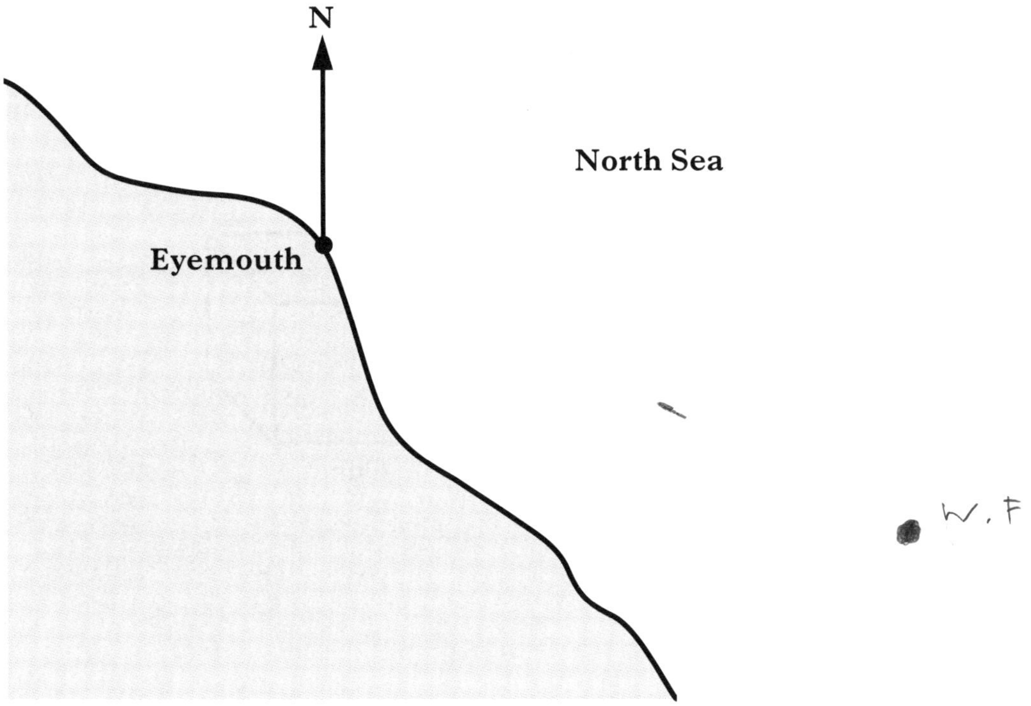

N

North Sea

Eyemouth

3

[Turn over for Question 14 on *Page sixteen*

Marks   KU   RE

14. The diagram below shows the net of a cube.

The total surface area of the cube is 150 square centimetres.

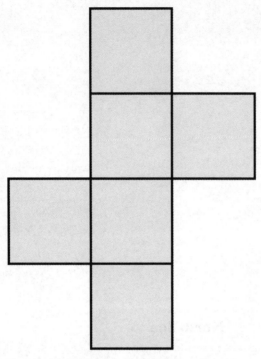

Net of Cube

Calculate the length of the side of the cube.

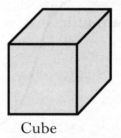

Cube

$15 \div 6 = 25$

$\sqrt{} \quad 25 = 5 \text{ cm}$

3

[END OF QUESTION PAPER]

ADDITIONAL SPACE FOR ANSWERS

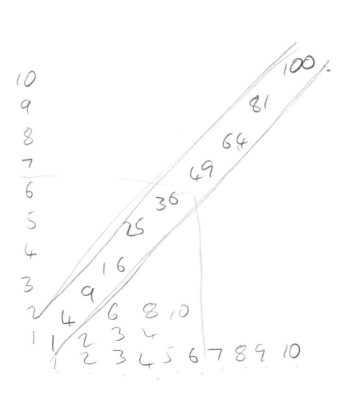

ADDITIONAL SPACE FOR ANSWERS

ADDITIONAL SPACE FOR ANSWERS

[BLANK PAGE]

[BLANK PAGE]

FOR OFFICIAL USE

G

KU   RE

Total marks

2500/403

NATIONAL
QUALIFICATIONS
2010

WEDNESDAY, 5 MAY
10.40 AM – 11.15 AM

MATHEMATICS
STANDARD GRADE
General Level
Paper 1
Non-calculator

Fill in these boxes and read what is printed below.

Full name of centre

Town

Forename(s)

Surname

Date of birth

Day   Month   Year   Scottish candidate number   Number of seat

1. **You may not use a calculator.**

2. Answer as many questions as you can.

3. Write your working and answers in the spaces provided. Additional space is provided at the end of this question-answer book for use if required. If you use this space, write clearly the number of the question involved.

4. Full credit will be given only where the solution contains appropriate working.

5. Before leaving the examination room you must give this book to the Invigilator. If you do not, you may lose all the marks for this paper.

FORMULAE LIST

Circumference of a circle: $C = \pi d$

Area of a circle: $A = \pi r^2$

Curved surface area of a cylinder: $A = 2\pi r h$

Volume of a cylinder: $V = \pi r^2 h$

Volume of a triangular prism: $V = Ah$

Theorem of Pythagoras:

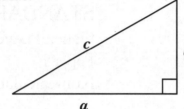

$$a^2 + b^2 = c^2$$

Trigonometric ratios
in a right angled
triangle:

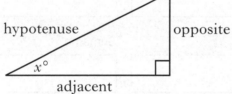

$$\tan x° = \frac{\text{opposite}}{\text{adjacent}}$$

$$\sin x° = \frac{\text{opposite}}{\text{hypotenuse}}$$

$$\cos x° = \frac{\text{adjacent}}{\text{hypotenuse}}$$

Gradient:

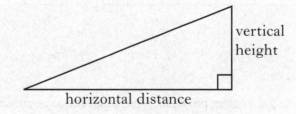

$$\text{Gradient} = \frac{\text{vertical height}}{\text{horizontal distance}}$$

Marks | KU | RE

1. Carry out the following calculations.

(a) $9{\cdot}32 - 5{\cdot}6 + 4{\cdot}27$

$$
\begin{array}{r}
{}^{8}9{\cdot}{}^{1}32 \\
-\ 5{\cdot}60 \\
\hline
3{\cdot}72 \\
+\ 4{\cdot}27 \\
\hline
7{\cdot}99
\end{array}
$$

1

(b) $37{\cdot}6 \times 8$

$$
\begin{array}{r}
37.6 \\
\times\ 8 \\
{}^{6}\ {}^{4} \\
\hline
300{\cdot}8
\end{array}
$$

1

(c) $2680 \div 400$

$$
\begin{array}{l}
6\ r\ 280 \\
400\overline{)2680} \\
\ -\ 2400 \qquad -6 \\
\hline
\ \ 0280 \qquad -
\end{array}
$$

1

(d) $7 \times 2\tfrac{1}{3}$

$\dfrac{3}{3} + \dfrac{3}{3} + \dfrac{1}{3}$

$(7 \times 2) + \left(7 \times \tfrac{1}{3}\right)$ $\dfrac{7 \times 7}{1 \times 3} = \dfrac{49}{3}$

$(7 \times 2) + \left(\tfrac{7}{1} \times \tfrac{1}{3}\right)$

$14\ +\ 2\tfrac{1}{3}$

$3\overline{)49}\ \ 16\ r\ 1\ \tfrac{1}{3}$

14

$2\tfrac{1}{3}$

$16\tfrac{1}{3}$

$\dfrac{1}{2} \times \dfrac{2}{1} = \dfrac{2}{2}$

$\dfrac{1}{2} \times \dfrac{4}{1}\ \ \dfrac{4}{2}$

2

[Turn over

Marks | KU | RE

2. The space shuttle programme costs $5800 million.

Write this number in scientific notation.

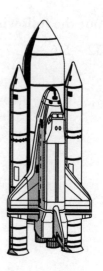

5.8,0₂0₃0₄0₅0₆,0,₇8₈9₉

$5·8 \times 10^9

2

3. One day last February, Anna compared the temperature in Edinburgh with the temperature in Montreal.

The temperature in Edinburgh was 8 °C.

The temperature in Montreal was –15 °C.

Find the difference between these temperatures.

−23°

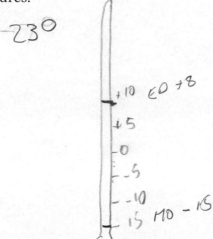

+10 E0 +8
+5
0
−5
−10
−15 M0 − 15

2

Marks   KU   RE

4. Complete this design so that the dotted line is an axis of symmetry.

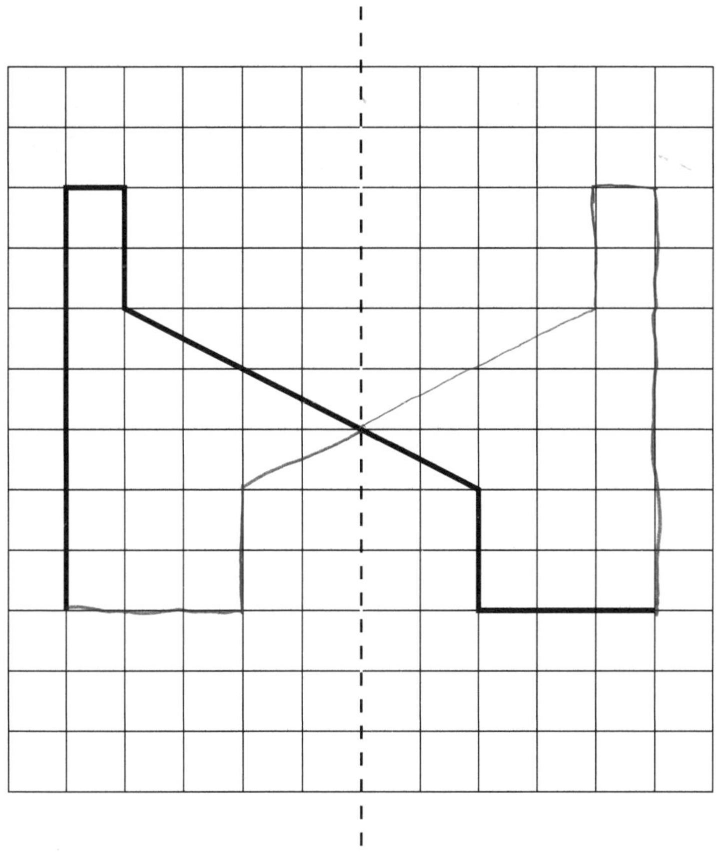

3

[Turn over

5. Karen asked her class to note the number of songs they downloaded to their phones in the last month.

The answers are shown below.

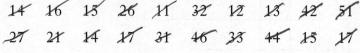

14 16 15 26 11 32 12 13 42 51

27 21 14 17 31 46 33 44 15 17

Display these answers in an ordered stem and leaf diagram.

```
10 | 1 2 3 4 4 5 5 6 7 7
20 | 1 6 7
30 | 1 2 3
40 | 2 4 6
50 | 1
```

3

Marks | KU | RE

6. Carla is laying a path in a nursery school.

She is using a mixture of alphabet tiles and coloured tiles.

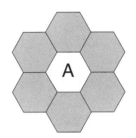

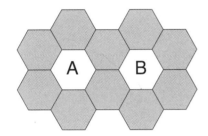

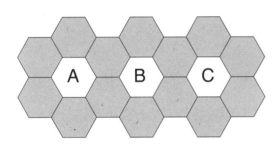

(*a*) Complete the table below.

Number of alphabet tiles (*a*)	1	2	3	4	5		12
Number of coloured tiles (*c*)	6	10	14	18	22		

2

(*b*) Write down a formula for calculating the number of coloured tiles (*c*) when you know the number of alphabet tiles (*a*).

$$c = (a \times 5) + 1$$

2

(*c*) Carla uses 86 coloured tiles to make the path.

How many alphabet tiles will be in the path?

2

Marks | KU | RE

7. When on holiday in Spain, Sandy sees a pair of jeans priced at 65 euros.

Sandy knows that he gets 13 euros for £10.

What is the price of the jeans in pounds?

65 euros

$$\begin{array}{r} 13 \\ \times 5 \\ \hline 65 \end{array}$$ convert to pounds =

£50

3

8. The price of a laptop is reduced from £400 to £320.

Calculate the percentage reduction in the price of the laptop.

~~£400~~
£320

25% because 80 × 5

3

Marks | KU | RE

9. The diagram shows a triangular prism.

The dimensions are given on the diagram.

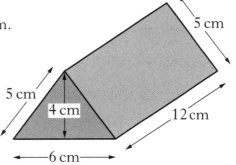

A **net** of this triangular prism is shown below.

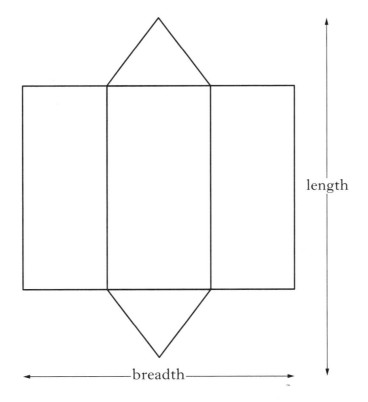

length

breadth

Calculate the length and breadth of this net.

breadth – 18cm
length – 20cm

2

[Turn over for Question 10 on *Page ten*

Marks | KU | RE

10.

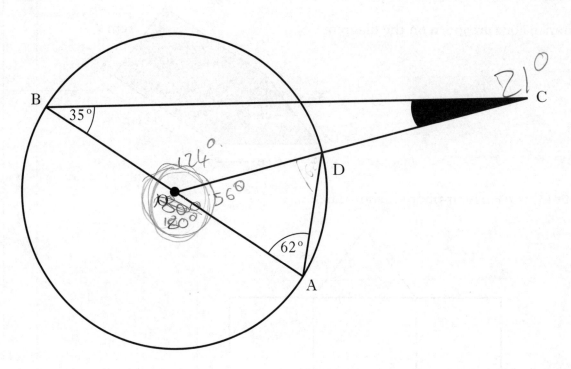

In the diagram above:

- ~~AB~~ is a diameter of the circle with centre O
- OC intersects the circle at D
- Angle ABC = 35°
- Angle BAD = 62°

Calculate the size of the shaded angle.

3

[*END OF QUESTION PAPER*]

ADDITIONAL SPACE FOR ANSWERS

$$\begin{array}{r} 180 \\ -\ 124 \\ \hline 056 \end{array}$$

180

$$\begin{array}{r} 3\overset{5}{\cancel{6}}0 \\ -\ 136 \\ \hline 224 \end{array}$$

$$\begin{array}{r} 3\overset{5}{\cancel{6}}0 \\ 236 \\ \hline 124 \end{array}$$

159

[BLANK PAGE]

FOR OFFICIAL USE

G

	KU	RE
Total marks		

2500/404

NATIONAL
QUALIFICATIONS
2010

WEDNESDAY, 5 MAY
11.35 AM – 12.30 PM

MATHEMATICS
STANDARD GRADE
General Level
Paper 2

Fill in these boxes and read what is printed below.

Full name of centre

Town

Forename(s)

Surname

Date of birth

Day   Month   Year   Scottish candidate number   Number of seat

1. **You may use a calculator.**

2. Answer as many questions as you can.

3. Write your working and answers in the spaces provided. Additional space is provided at the end of this question-answer book for use if required. If you use this space, write clearly the number of the question involved.

4. Full credit will be given only where the solution contains appropriate working.

5. Before leaving the examination room you must give this book to the Invigilator. If you do not, you may lose all the marks for this paper.

FORMULAE LIST

Circumference of a circle: $\qquad$ $C = \pi d$

Area of a circle: $\qquad$ $A = \pi r^2$

Curved surface area of a cylinder: $\qquad$ $A = 2\pi r h$

Volume of a cylinder: $\qquad$ $V = \pi r^2 h$

Volume of a triangular prism: $\qquad$ $V = Ah$

Theorem of Pythagoras:

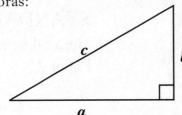

$$a^2 + b^2 = c^2$$

Trigonometric ratios
in a right angled
triangle:

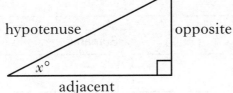

$$\tan x^\circ = \frac{\text{opposite}}{\text{adjacent}}$$

$$\sin x^\circ = \frac{\text{opposite}}{\text{hypotenuse}}$$

$$\cos x^\circ = \frac{\text{adjacent}}{\text{hypotenuse}}$$

Gradient:

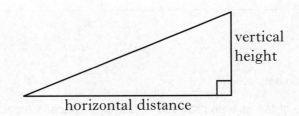

$$\text{Gradient} = \frac{\text{vertical height}}{\text{horizontal distance}}$$

Marks

KU | RE

1. Ten people were asked to guess the number of coffee beans in a jar.

   Their guesses were:

   310 260 198 250 275 300 245 225 310 200

   (a) What is the range of this data?

   $$310 - 198 = \boxed{112}$$

   1

   (b) Find the median.

   $$310 + 260 + 198 + 250 + 275$$
   $$+ 300 + 245 + 225 + 310$$
   $$+ 200 = 2573 \div 10 =$$

   2

   $$257.3$$

   [Turn over

Marks | KU | RE

2. Mr and Mrs Kapela book a cruise to Bruges for themselves and their three children.

- They depart on 27 June

  Mr and Mrs Kapela share an outside cabin and their three children share an inside cabin

  There is a 20% discount for each child

Calculate the total cost of the cruise.

Mini Cruise to Bruges, Belgium		
	Price per person	
Departure Date	Inside Cabin (£)	Outside Cabin (£)
16 May	236	250
30 May	244	274
13 June	266	300
27 June	275	310
12 July	291	325
26 July	312	355
9 Aug	327	370

$310 \times 2 = 620$

$275 \div 10 = 27.5 \times 2 = 55$

$55 \times 3 = 165$

$165 + 620 = £785$

3

Marks

KU	RE

3. As part of his healthy diet, Tomas has decided to buy fruit in his weekly shopping.

His favourite fruits and their costs per pack are given in the table below.

Fruit	Cost
Apples	£1·25
Oranges	£1·20
Grapes	£2·49
Pears	£1·56
Melon	£1·98

He wants to

- buy 3 different packs of fruit

- spend a maximum of £5 on fruit.

One possible selection and its cost are shown in the table below.

Complete the table to show all of Tomas's possible selections and their cost.

Apples	Oranges	Grapes	Pears	Melon	Cost
✓	✓		✓		£4·01
✓	✓			✓	£4.43
✓	✓	✓			£4.94
✓	✓		✓	✓	£4.74
✓			✓	✓	£4.79

4

[Turn over

Marks | KU | RE

4. (*a*) Complete the table below for $y = 2x - 3$.

x	−1	1	3
y	-2 -3=-5	2-3=-1	6-3=3

2

(*b*) Using the table in part (*a*), draw the graph of the line $y = 2x - 3$ on the grid below.

2×0 -3 = -3

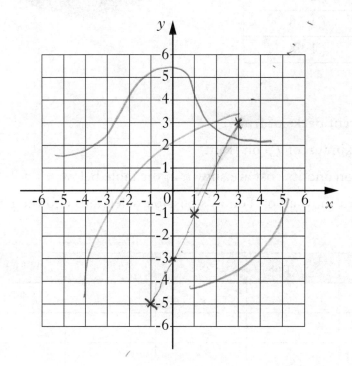

2

DO NOT WRITE IN THIS MARGIN

Marks | KU | RE

5. For safety reasons the speed limit outside Fairfield Park is 20 miles per hour.

The distance between the speed limit signs outside Fairfield Park is half a mile.

A van took 2 minutes to travel between these signs.

Was the van travelling at a safe speed?

Give a reason for your answer.

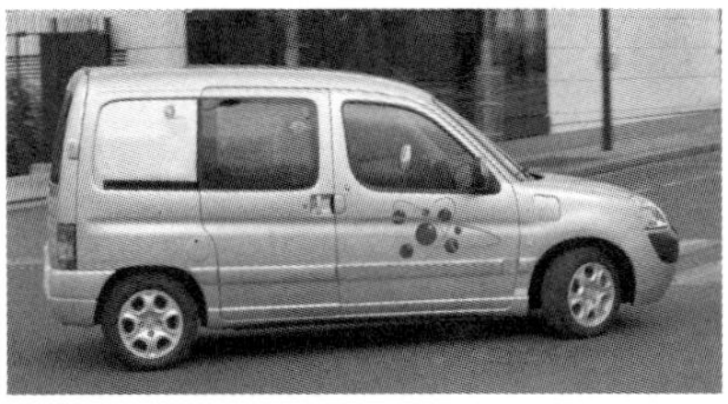

yes, At 15 mph

3

[Turn over

DO NOT WRITE IN THIS MARGIN

Marks | KU | RE

6. (*a*) Simplify

$8(c - 3) + 5(c + 2).$

13 x (c − 1)

3

(*b*) Solve algebraically

$25 = 7x + 4.$

25 − 4 = 21
21 = 7x
21 ÷ 7 = 3

2

Marks | KU | RE

7. Rowan wants to buy 13 theatre tickets.

The price of one ticket is £12·50.

The theatre has a special online offer of four tickets for the price of three.

Rowan makes use of the special online offer.

How much does Rowan pay for the 13 theatre tickets?

Online Ticket Offer
4 for the price of 3

$$\begin{array}{r} 12.50 \\ \times 3 \\ \hline 37.50 \end{array}$$

$$\begin{array}{r} 37.50 \\ \times 3 \\ \hline 112.50 \end{array}$$

$$\begin{array}{r} 112.50 \\ + 12.50 \\ \hline £125.00 \end{array}$$

3

[Turn over

Marks | KU | RE

8. A survey of 1800 first time voters was carried out.

The pie chart below shows how they would vote at the next election.

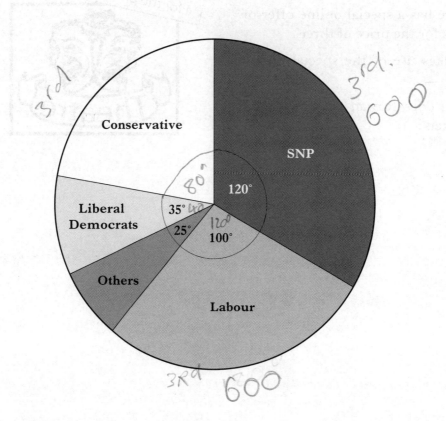

How many of the 1800 first time voters would vote Conservative?

400

3

Marks | KU | RE

9. A tennis court is 11 metres wide.

It has an area of 264 square metres.

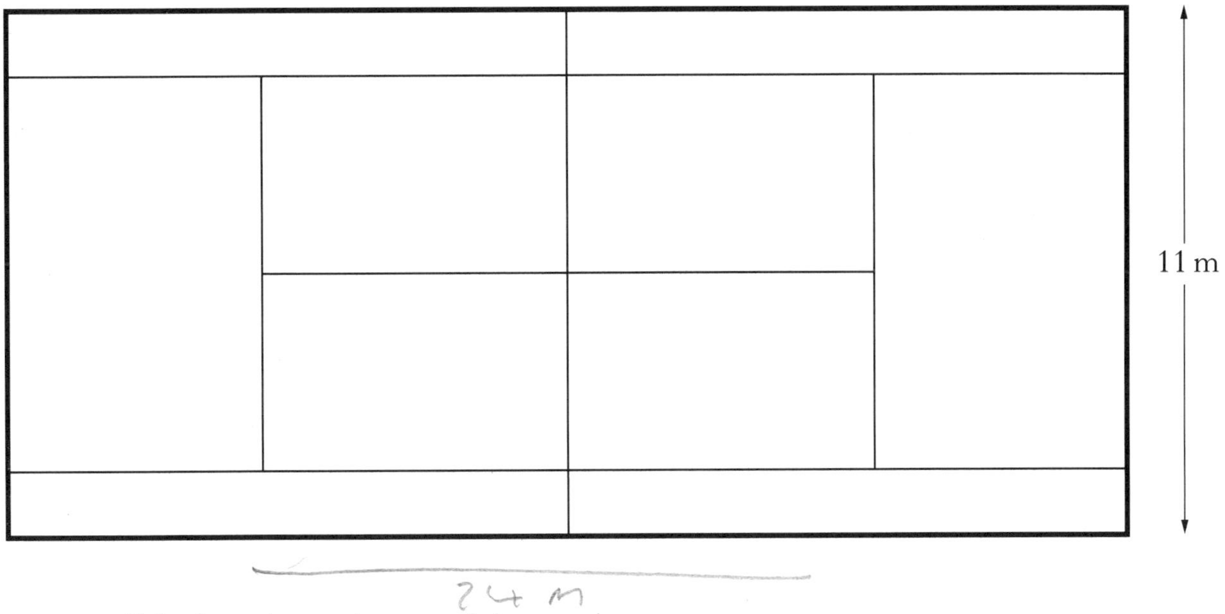

11 m

24 M

Calculate the perimeter of the tennis court.

70 m

3

[Turn over

Marks | KU | RE

10. Ahmed is making a frame to strengthen a stairway in a shopping centre.

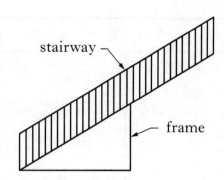

He needs to know the angle the stairway makes with the floor, as shown in the diagram below.

The hypotenuse of the frame is 5·2 m and the horizontal distance is 4·5 m.

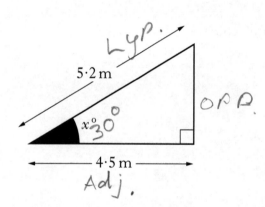

27.04
20.25

Calculate the size of the shaded angle $x°$.

3

Marks | KU | RE

11. A climber needs to be rescued.

His position from the helicopter base is marked on the map.

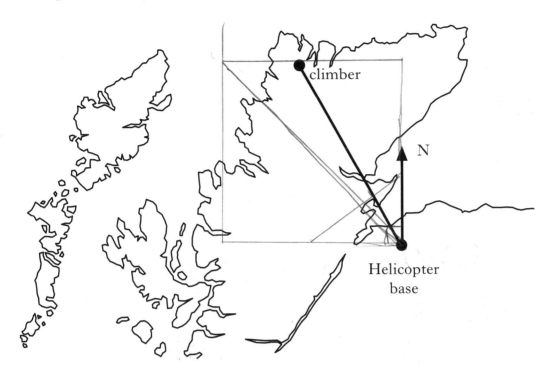

climber

N

Helicopter
base

(*a*) Using a scale of 1 centimetre to 15 kilometres, calculate the distance of
the climber from the helicopter base.

82.5 km

1

(*b*) Find the bearing of the climber from the helicopter base.

NNW

2

[Turn over

Marks | KU | RE

12. An earring in the shape of an isosceles triangle is made from silver wire.

The dimensions of the earring are shown on the diagram below.

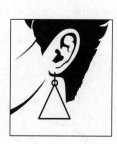

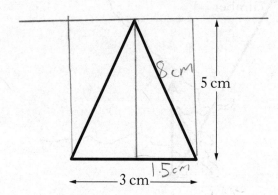

8 cm

5 cm

3 cm — 1.5 cm

Calculate the length of silver wire needed to make a **pair** of earrings.

Do not use a scale drawing.

38 cm

4

Marks | KU | RE

13. A plastic speed bump in the shape of a half cylinder is used to slow traffic outside a Primary School.

The speed bump has radius of 10 centimetres and a length of 7 metres as shown in the diagram below.

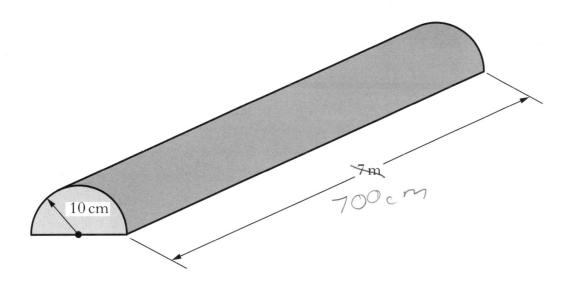

10 cm

7 m

700 cm

Calculate the volume of plastic used to make the speed bump.

$1099.55 \, m^2$

3

[Turn over for Question 14 on *Page sixteen*

Marks | KU | RE

14. Liam buys a new stereo using the monthly payment plan.

The cash price of the stereo is £360.

The total cost of the monthly payment plan is **5% more than the cash price**.

Liam pays a deposit of one fifth of the cash price followed by 30 equal monthly payments.

Cash Price £360

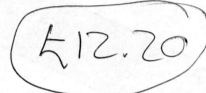

Monthly Payment Plan
Deposit ⅕ of cash price
and 30 monthly payments

How much will Liam pay each month?

£72

£12.20

$$30\overline{)378}$$
300 − 10
——
78
60 − 2
18

10 6 6
12 6

0.20
$$30\overline{)6.0000}$$

4

[END OF QUESTION PAPER]

[BLANK PAGE]

FOR OFFICIAL USE

G

	KU	RE
Paper 1		
Paper 2		
Total		

2500/403

NATIONAL
QUALIFICATIONS
2011

WEDNESDAY, 4 MAY
10.40 AM – 11.15 AM

MATHEMATICS
STANDARD GRADE
General Level
Paper 1
Non-calculator

Fill in these boxes and read what is printed below.

Full name of centre

Town

Forename(s)

Surname

Date of birth

Day   Month   Year   Scottish candidate number   Number of seat

1. **You may not use a calculator.**

2. Answer as many questions as you can.

3. Write your working and answers in the spaces provided. Additional space is provided at the end of this question-answer book for use if required. If you use this space, write clearly the number of the question involved.

4. Full credit will be given only where the solution contains appropriate working.

5. Before leaving the examination room you must give this book to the Invigilator. If you do not, you may lose all the marks for this paper.

FORMULAE LIST

Circumference of a circle: $\quad C = \pi d$

Area of a circle: $\quad A = \pi r^2$

Curved surface area of a cylinder: $\quad A = 2\pi rh$

Volume of a cylinder: $\quad V = \pi r^2 h$

Volume of a triangular prism: $\quad V = Ah$

Theorem of Pythagoras:

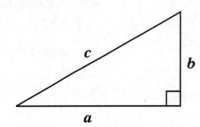

$$a^2 + b^2 = c^2$$

Trigonometric ratios
in a right angled
triangle:

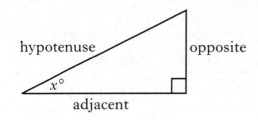

$$\tan x^\circ = \frac{\text{opposite}}{\text{adjacent}}$$

$$\sin x^\circ = \frac{\text{opposite}}{\text{hypotenuse}}$$

$$\cos x^\circ = \frac{\text{adjacent}}{\text{hypotenuse}}$$

Gradient:

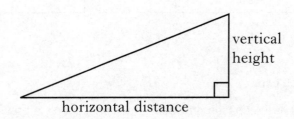

$$\text{Gradient} = \frac{\text{vertical height}}{\text{horizontal distance}}$$

Marks | KU | RE

1. Carry out the following calculations.

(a) $437 \cdot 5 - 95 \cdot 61$

$$\begin{array}{r} 437.50 \\ - 95.61 \\ \hline 341.89 \end{array}$$

1

(b) $18 \cdot 4 \times 700$

$18.4 \times 100 = 1840.0$

$$\begin{array}{r} 1840 \\ \times 7 \\ \hline 12880.0 \end{array}$$

1

(c) $0 \cdot 258 \div 6$

0.043

$6 \overline{)0.258}$

1

(d) Find $\frac{2}{3}$ of 24

$\frac{1}{3} 24 = 8$ so $2 \times 8 = 16$

2

[Turn over

DO NOT WRITE IN THIS MARGIN

Marks | KU | RE

2. The thickness of a hair on Robbie's head is 0·00254 centimetres.

Write 0·00254 in scientific notation. 2

~~254~~

2.54×10^{-3}

Marks | KU | RE

3. Margaret is working on the design for a gold bracelet.

She is using gold lengths to make each section.

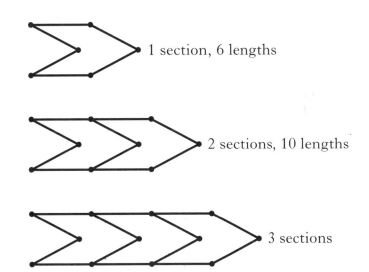

1 section, 6 lengths

2 sections, 10 lengths

3 sections

(a) Complete the table below.

Number of sections (s)	1	2	3	4		10
Number of gold lengths (g)	6	10	14	18		42

2

(b) Write down a formula for calculating the number of gold lengths, (g), when you know the number of sections (s).

$g = (s \times 6)$ $g = (6s + s) - 1$

2

(c) Margaret uses 66 gold lengths to make a bracelet.

How many sections does this bracelet contain?

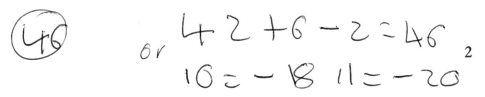

46   or $42 + 6 - 2 = 46$

$10 = -8$ $11 = -20$

2

[Turn over

Marks   KU   RE

4. Sean draws a stem and leaf diagram to display charity donations.

Donation (£)

```
0 | 3   5   8
1 | 0   0   0   2   2
2 | 2   4   8
3 | 0   5   5   6   8   8
4 | 0   0   5
```

n = 20   4 | 5 represents £45

Using the above diagram, find:

(a)   the mode;

1

(b)   the median;

2

(c)   the range of the donations.

1

Marks | KU | RE

5. The diagram below shows a large rectangle that has been divided into 3 small rectangles.

The small rectangles are labelled A, B and C.

Some of the dimensions are given on the diagram.

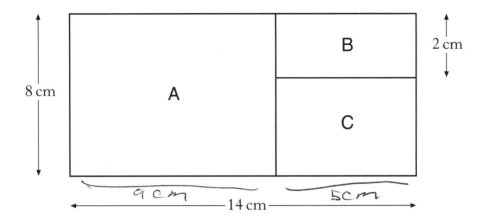

Rectangle B has an area of 10 square centimetres.

Calculate the area of rectangle A.

$$2 \times 5 = 10$$

$$9 \times 8 = 72$$

$$\boxed{72 \, cm^2}$$

4

[Turn over

Marks   KU   RE

6. Tom compared the temperatures in the Sahara Desert and at the North Pole.

The temperature in the Sahara Desert was 32 °C.

The temperature at the North Pole was 46 °C less than the temperature in the Sahara Desert.

What was the temperature at the North Pole?

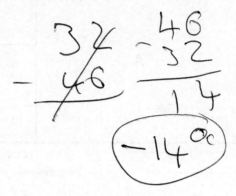

2

7. In the diagram:

- ABCD is a kite
- Angle DAB = 50°
- Angle DBC = 30°

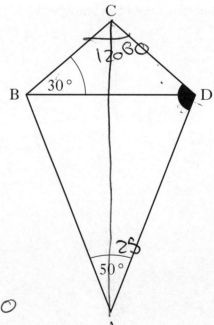

Calculate the size of shaded angle ADC.

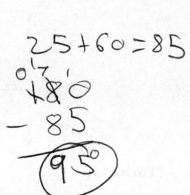

3

Marks | KU | RE

8.

Urban Wildlife Park

Admission Charges	
Adult	£13·50
Children aged 3 and under	£10·75
Children aged 4 to 16	£11·50
Family Ticket (1 Adult & 2 Children)	£32·00
Family Ticket (2 Adults & 2 Children)	£42·00
Family Ticket (2 Adults & 3 Children)	£51·00

Alan and Kate take their 12 year old twin daughters to the Urban Wildlife Park.

Instead of buying four individual tickets, they decide to buy a Family Ticket.

How much money do they save?

$2 \times £11.50 = £23$

$2 \times £13.50 = £27$

$+ £50$

£50 £42

$£50 - £42 = £8$

3

[Turn over for Question 9 on *Page ten*

Marks | KU | RE

9. Three steel nails are shown below.

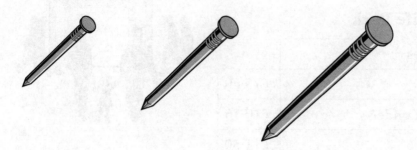

The lengths of the nails are in the ratio 1 : 3 : 5.

The length of the middle nail is 7·5 centimetres.

Calculate the length of the large nail.

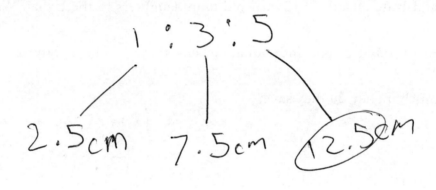

3

[END OF QUESTION PAPER]

ADDITIONAL SPACE FOR ANSWERS

[BLANK PAGE]

FOR OFFICIAL USE

KU   RE

G

2500/404

NATIONAL
QUALIFICATIONS
2011

WEDNESDAY, 4 MAY
11.35 AM – 12.30 PM

MATHEMATICS
STANDARD GRADE
General Level
Paper 2

Fill in these boxes and read what is printed below.

Full name of centre

Town

Forename(s)

Surname

Date of birth

Day	Month	Year	Scottish candidate number	Number of seat

1. **You may use a calculator.**

2. Answer as many questions as you can.

3. Write your working and answers in the spaces provided. Additional space is provided at the end of this question-answer book for use if required. If you use this space, write clearly the number of the question involved.

4. Full credit will be given only where the solution contains appropriate working.

5. Before leaving the examination room you must give this book to the Invigilator. If you do not, you may lose all the marks for this paper.

FORMULAE LIST

Circumference of a circle: $\qquad$ $C = \pi d$
Area of a circle: $\qquad$ $A = \pi r^2$
Curved surface area of a cylinder: $\qquad$ $A = 2\pi rh$
Volume of a cylinder: $\qquad$ $V = \pi r^2 h$
Volume of a triangular prism: $\qquad$ $V = Ah$

Theorem of Pythagoras:

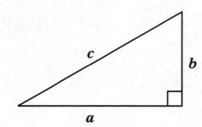

$$a^2 + b^2 = c^2$$

Trigonometric ratios
in a right angled
triangle:

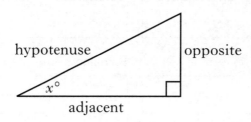

$$\tan x^\circ = \frac{\text{opposite}}{\text{adjacent}}$$

$$\sin x^\circ = \frac{\text{opposite}}{\text{hypotenuse}}$$

$$\cos x^\circ = \frac{\text{adjacent}}{\text{hypotenuse}}$$

Gradient:

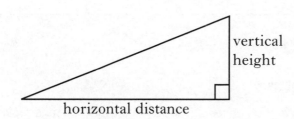

$$\text{Gradient} = \frac{\text{vertical height}}{\text{horizontal distance}}$$

Marks | KU | RE

1. Tariq has a £216 000 mortgage.

The interest rate on this mortgage is 4·5% per annum.

How much does Tariq pay in interest **each month**?

3

[Turn over

DO NOT WRITE IN THIS MARGIN

Marks KU RE

2. There are 2 yellow, 3 red, 1 blue and 4 orange cubes in a bag.

(*a*) Jason takes a cube from the bag.

What is the probability that it is orange?

2 in 3

1

(*b*) The cube is replaced in the bag and 3 white cubes are added to the bag.

What is the probability that the next cube taken from the bag is **not** red?

10 3

~~7 in 10~~

7 in 10

2

Marks | KU | RE

3. Andrew is on holiday in Canada and has 600 Canadian Dollars.

He spends 565 Canadian Dollars during his holiday.

At the end of his holiday he changes the remaining Canadian Dollars to Pounds.

The exchange rate is £1 = 1·74 Canadian Dollars.

How much will he receive?

$$\begin{array}{r} 600 \\ - 565 \\ \hline 035 \end{array}$$

$$35 \div 1.74 =$$

$$£20.11$$

$$£20.11$$

3

Marks | KU | RE

4. For the school gala day the maths teachers have invented a game.

To play the game each person throws **three** bean bags at the target.

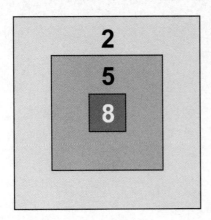

Score
8 points for hitting the "Centre" part
5 points for hitting the "Middle" part
2 points for hitting the "Outer" part

All three bean bags must hit the target to win a prize.

Prizes are won for **15 points or more**.

Complete the table below to show all the different ways to win a prize.

Number of bean bags scoring 8 points	Number of bean bags scoring 5 points	Number of bean bags scoring 2 points	Total Points
2	0	1	18
0	3	0	15
1	1	1	15
3	0	0	24
1	2	0	18
2	1	0	21

4

Marks KU RE

5. Millie and her friends are going hillwalking.

Millie tells her friends that they will start their walk by heading Southwest.

(*a*) What is the three-figure bearing for Southwest?

225°

1

Later on, Millie tells her friends that they need to walk on a bearing of 135°.

(*b*) What direction is represented by a bearing of 135°? Southeast

1

[Turn over

DO NOT WRITE IN THIS MARGIN

Marks KU RE

6. (*a*) Factorise fully

$$18 + 12t.$$

2

(*b*) Solve algebraically

$$5m - 3 = 37 + m.$$

3

Marks | KU | RE

7. Sally can record and store television programmes using her TV plus system.

The display on her system shows

TVplus
✦ Maximum storage: **80 hours**
✦ Remaining storage: **13%**

- maximum storage space 80 hours

- storage space remaining 13%.

The new TV series of "City Life" has 12 episodes each lasting 55 minutes.

Can she record the whole of the "City Life" series on the remaining storage space?

Give a reason for your answer.

$$80 \times 60$$

$$4800 \text{ mins}$$

$$4800 \div 100 = 48$$

$$\times 13$$
$$144$$
$$4.80$$
$$624 \text{ mins}$$

4

[**Turn over**

$$55 \times 12$$
$$110$$
$$550$$
$$660$$

624 mins left
series = 660 mins
no. Sally is not able
to record the full
series

Marks | KU | RE

8. Complete this shape so that it has half-turn symmetry about O.

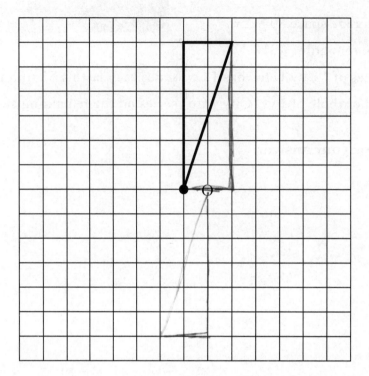

2

Marks | KU | RE

9. Larry has invented a device for checking that ladders are positioned at the correct angle.

His design for the device is given below.

Calculate the size of the shaded angle.

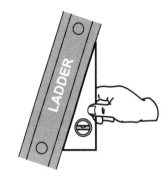

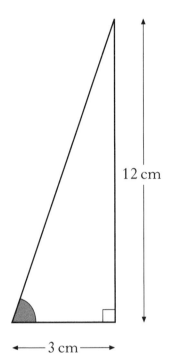

12 cm

←—— 3 cm ——→

3

[Turn over

Marks KU RE

10. Vicky makes a number of deliveries in her van.

When the van is moving the on-board computer records the total distance and the average speed.

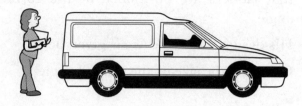

Last Wednesday the computer recorded

- distance = 162 miles

- average speed = 36 miles per hour.

Including stops, Vicky took 6 hours 55 minutes to complete her deliveries.

For how long was Vicky's van stationary?

4

Marks KU RE

11. (*a*) On the grid below, plot the points P (–7, –3) and Q (5, 6).

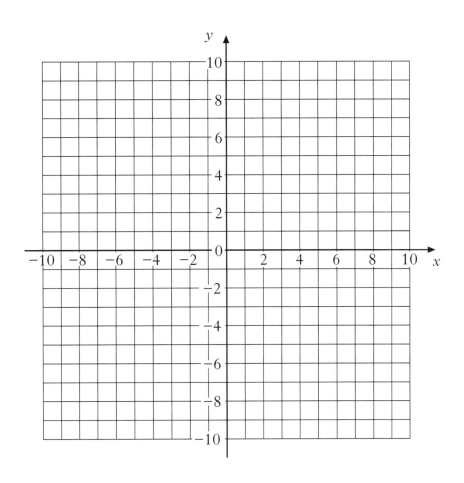

1

(*b*) Find the gradient of line PQ.

2

[Turn over

12. A warning sign is in the shape of an isosceles triangle.

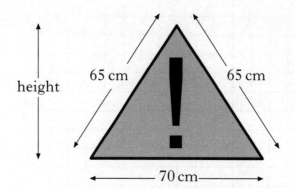

Calculate the height of the sign.

4

DO NOT WRITE IN THIS MARGIN

Marks KU RE

13. Helen has recorded the scores for her last eighteen games of golf.

Her scores are shown below.

Score	*Frequency*	*Score* × *Frequency*
69	3	
70	2	
71	4	
72	4	
73	2	
74	1	
75	2	
	Total = 18	Total =

Complete the above table and find Helen's **mean** score per game.

Round your answer to 1 decimal place. **4**

[Turn over for Question 14 on *Page sixteen*

DO NOT
WRITE IN
THIS
MARGIN

KU	RE

14. Alex uses a circular piece of wood to make a measuring wheel.

The wheel has a radius of 18 centimetres.

How many complete metres are measured by 15 rotations of the wheel?

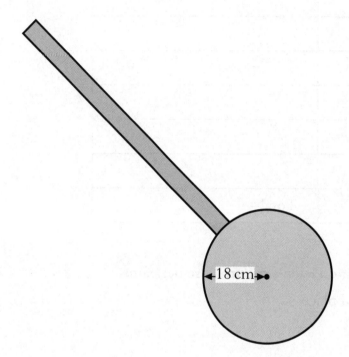

◄18 cm►

4

[END OF QUESTION PAPER]

STANDARD GRADE | GENERAL

2012

[BLANK PAGE]

FOR OFFICIAL USE

	KU	RE
Paper 1		
Paper 2		
Total		

G

2500/29/01

NATIONAL
QUALIFICATIONS
2012

WEDNESDAY, 2 MAY
10.40 AM – 11.15 AM

MATHEMATICS
STANDARD GRADE
General Level
Paper 1
Non-calculator

Fill in these boxes and read what is printed below.

Full name of centre

Town

Forename(s)

Surname

Date of birth

Day   Month   Year   Scottish candidate number   Number of seat

1 You may **not** use a calculator.

2 Answer as many questions as you can.

3 Write your working and answers in the spaces provided. Additional space is provided at the end of this question-answer book for use if required. If you use this space, write clearly the number of the question involved.

4 Full credit will be given only where the solution contains appropriate working.

5 Before leaving the examination room you must give this book to the Invigilator. If you do not, you may lose all the marks for this paper.

FORMULAE LIST

Circumference of a circle: $C = \pi d$
Area of a circle: $A = \pi r^2$
Curved surface area of a cylinder: $A = 2\pi rh$
Volume of a cylinder: $V = \pi r^2 h$
Volume of a triangular prism: $V = Ah$

Theorem of Pythagoras:

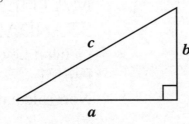

$$a^2 + b^2 = c^2$$

Trigonometric ratios
in a right angled
triangle:

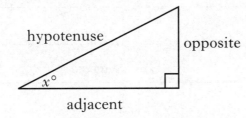

$$\tan x^\circ = \frac{\text{opposite}}{\text{adjacent}}$$

$$\sin x^\circ = \frac{\text{opposite}}{\text{hypotenuse}}$$

$$\cos x^\circ = \frac{\text{adjacent}}{\text{hypotenuse}}$$

Gradient:

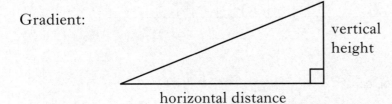

$$\text{Gradient} = \frac{\text{vertical height}}{\text{horizontal distance}}$$

DO NOT WRITE IN THIS MARGIN

Marks KU RE

1. Carry out the following calculations.

(*a*) 14·6 – 3·21 + 5·3 **1**

(*b*) 2·44 × 90 **1**

(*c*) 76·8 ÷ 6 **1**

(*d*) $\frac{1}{4} + \frac{1}{3}$ **2**

[Turn over

Marks

KU | RE

2. Top footballers can earn £27·2 million each year.

Write 27·2 million in scientific notation.

2

3. An amusement arcade has a lighting effect in the shape of triangles with coloured lights attached.

The lighting effect can be assembled in sections as shown below.

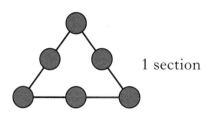 1 section

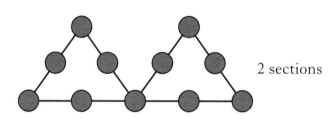 2 sections

(a) Complete the table below.

Number of sections (s)	1	2	3	4	5		12
Number of coloured lights (c)	6	11					

2

(b) Write down a formula for calculating the number of coloured lights (c) when you know the number of sections (s).

2

(c) The amusement arcade's lighting effect uses a total of 116 coloured lights.

How many sections are in the lighting effect?

2

[Turn over

Marks

KU | RE

4. From the numbers 50, 93, 43, 56, 85, 42 choose:

(*a*) two numbers which are multiples of seven;

1

(*b*) the prime number;

1

(*c*) the number which is closest to a square number.

1

Marks | KU | RE

5. A website shows some extreme temperatures recorded on Earth.

The highest temperature recorded was 58 °C in Libya in 1922.

The lowest temperature recorded was −64 °C in Siberia in 1973.

Find the difference between these two temperatures.

2

6. Starting with the smallest, write the following in order.

$$\frac{1}{5} \qquad 0{\cdot}05 \qquad 51\% \qquad 0{\cdot}505 \qquad \frac{5}{10}$$

2

[Turn over

Marks KU RE

7. Colin works in a supermarket at the weekend.

He is paid the basic rate of £7·50 per hour on Saturdays.

He is paid at time and a half on Sundays.

Last weekend he worked 7 hours on Saturday and 6 hours on Sunday.

Calculate Colin's total pay for last weekend.

3

Marks | KU | RE

8. 720 people were at The Venue on Friday.

On Friday, it was only 80% full.

On Saturday, The Venue was full.

How many people were at The Venue on Saturday?

3

[Turn over

Marks | KU | R

9. Jamie took the overnight sleeper train from Edinburgh to London.

   She arrived in London at 0624.

   Her journey had taken 6 hours 58 minutes.

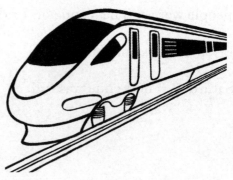

   When did Jamie's sleeper train leave Edinburgh?

2

Marks | KU | RE

10.

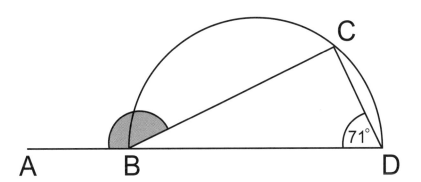

The diagram above shows a semi-circle with BD as diameter.

- C lies on the circumference

- In triangle BCD, angle CDB is 71°

- AD is a straight line

Calculate the size of the shaded angle ABC.

3

[END OF QUESTION PAPER]

ADDITIONAL SPACE FOR ANSWERS

FOR OFFICIAL USE

KU	RE

G

2500/29/02

NATIONAL
QUALIFICATIONS
2012

WEDNESDAY, 2 MAY
11.35 AM – 12.30 PM

MATHEMATICS
STANDARD GRADE
General Level
Paper 2

Fill in these boxes and read what is printed below.

Full name of centre

Town

Forename(s)

Surname

Date of birth

Day   Month   Year   Scottish candidate number   Number of seat

---

1 **You may use a calculator.**

2 Answer as many questions as you can.

3 Write your working and answers in the spaces provided. Additional space is provided at the end of this question-answer book for use if required. If you use this space, write clearly the number of the question involved.

4 Full credit will be given only where the solution contains appropriate working.

5 Before leaving the examination room you must give this book to the Invigilator. If you do not, you may lose all the marks for this paper.

FORMULAE LIST

Circumference of a circle: $C = \pi d$
Area of a circle: $A = \pi r^2$
Curved surface area of a cylinder: $A = 2\pi rh$
Volume of a cylinder: $V = \pi r^2 h$
Volume of a triangular prism: $V = Ah$

Theorem of Pythagoras:

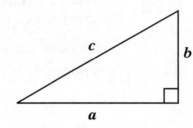

$$a^2 + b^2 = c^2$$

Trigonometric ratios
in a right angled
triangle:

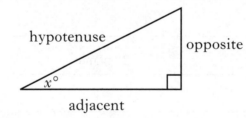

$$\tan x° = \frac{\text{opposite}}{\text{adjacent}}$$

$$\sin x° = \frac{\text{opposite}}{\text{hypotenuse}}$$

$$\cos x° = \frac{\text{adjacent}}{\text{hypotenuse}}$$

Gradient:

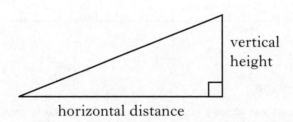

$$\text{Gradient} = \frac{\text{vertical height}}{\text{horizontal distance}}$$

DO NOT WRITE IN THIS MARGIN

Marks | KU | RE

1. In the Annual Fun Run, Lucy ran 12 kilometres in 1 hour 15 minutes.

Calculate her average speed in kilometres per hour.

3

[Turn over

Marks | KU | R

2. John has drawn this design.

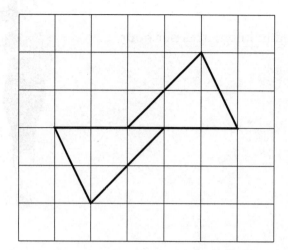

Using a scale factor of 2, draw an enlargement of John's design on the grid below.

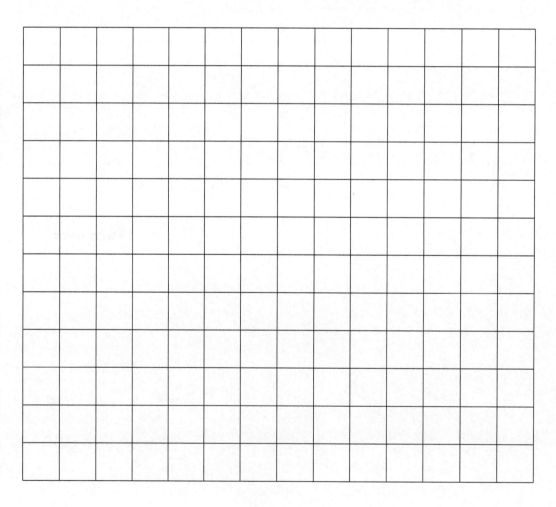

3

3. Stephen is buying new kitchen cabinets.

Kitchen Cabinet Price List	Width		
Cabinets	30 cm	50 cm	80 cm
Base	£43	£66	£94
Wall	£39	£58	£92
High	£68	£116	£170
Drawer	£103	£123	£179

He buys:

- three Base cabinets of width 50 centimetres
- two Wall cabinets of width 30 centimetres
- one Drawer cabinet of width 80 centimetres.

Calculate the total cost of his kitchen cabinets.

3

[Turn over

Marks | KU | RE

4. Brian sets out from camp during an expedition.

The arrow in the sketch below shows the direction in which he is travelling.

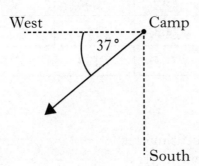

What is the three-figure bearing of this direction?

2

5. Renvi is tiling her bathroom floor.

She needs 15 boxes of tiles.

The price of one box is £23.

The tile shop has a special offer of "**buy one box get one box half price**".

Renvi makes use of the special offer.

How much does Renvi pay for 15 boxes of tiles?

4

[Turn over

Marks | KU | RE

6. (a) Complete the table below for $y = 2x - 1$.

x	−1	1	3
y			

2

(b) Using the table in part (a), draw the graph of the line $y = 2x - 1$ on the grid below.

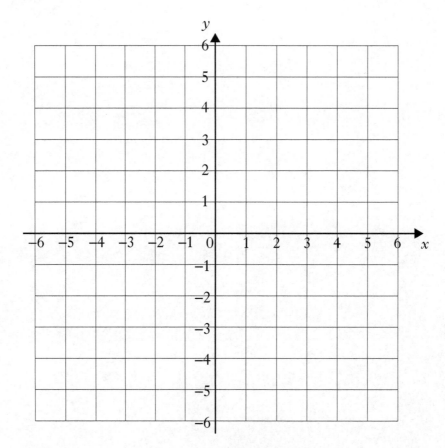

2

7. Maggie has bought a garden shed.

The dimensions for one side of the shed are shown in the diagram below.

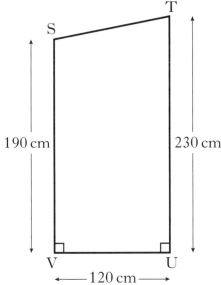

Calculate the length of ST.

Do not use a scale drawing.

4

[Turn over

Marks | KU | RI

8. The cash price of a 3D TV at Curlys Superstore is £1315.

Curlys also has an interest free payment plan.

The payment plan is a deposit plus twelve equal monthly payments.

The deposit for the TV is £175.

Find the cost of the monthly payments.

3

DO NOT WRITE IN THIS MARGIN

Marks	KU	RE

9. (*a*) Solve algebraically

$$6(2x - 3) = 42.$$

3

(*b*) Factorise

$$12t + 9u.$$

2

[Turn over

Marks KU RI

10. At the World Athletics Championships the mean time for the first semi-final of the 100 metres was 9·98 seconds.

For the second semi-final the times, in seconds, were:

10·21   10·04   9·92   9·98   10·04   9·94   9·9   9·73.

Was the mean time for the second semi-final better than the mean time for the first semi-final?

Give a reason for your answer.

4

Marks KU RE

11. The pupils in fourth year at Wanlockhead High School voted in the school election.

The votes for each candidate are given below:

Eco:	86 votes
Health:	24 votes
Fairtrade:	52 votes
Community:	18 votes

Using a suitable scale, draw a bar chart to show this information.

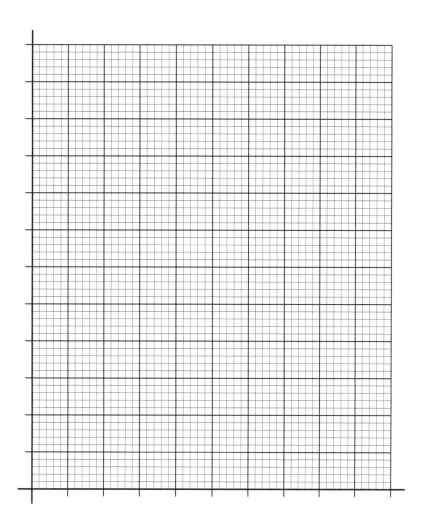

No. of votes

Candidate

4

[Turn over

12. The Olympic symbol consists of five identical circles.

Part of the symbol is shown in the diagram below.

- the length of the symbol is 45 centimetres
- the circles are equally spaced
- the gap between the adjacent circles is 1·5 centimetres.

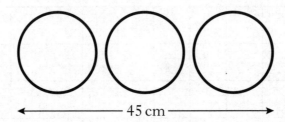

←————— 45 cm —————→

Calculate the radius of a circle.

3

Marks | KU | RE

13. A surveyor has to calculate the height of a mobile phone mast.

From a point 20 metres from the base of the mast, the angle of elevation to the top is 52°.

Calculate the height of the mobile phone mast.

Round your answer to 1 decimal place.

Do not use a scale drawing.

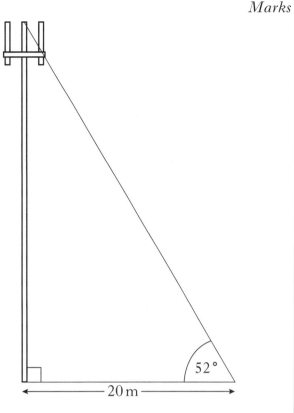

4

[**Turn over for Question 14 on** *Page sixteen*

Marks KU RF

14. Pachuri Sauces are changing the shape of the labels on their jars from circles to squares.

The labels have the same area.

The circle has a radius of 4·5 centimetres.

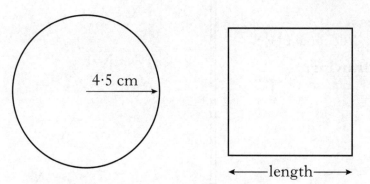

4·5 cm

←——length——→

Calculate the length of the new square label.

3

[END OF QUESTION PAPER]

ADDITIONAL SPACE FOR ANSWERS

ADDITIONAL SPACE FOR ANSWERS

ADDITIONAL SPACE FOR ANSWERS

[BLANK PAGE]

STANDARD GRADE | ANSWER SECTION

SQA STANDARD GRADE
GENERAL MATHEMATICS 2008–2012

MATHEMATICS GENERAL PAPER 1 2008 (NON-CALCULATOR)

1. (a) 14·17

   (b) 57·51

   (c) 0·0437

   (d) 350

2. 4 500 000

3. (a) and (b)

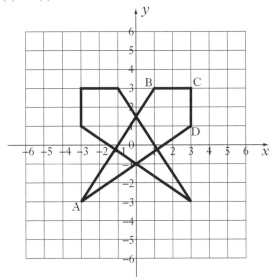

4. $1·04 \times 10^7$

5. (a) 1238, 1247, 1256, 2345

   (b) 2345

6. $-9, -8, 7$

7. £1·22

8. (a) $\frac{2}{3}$

   (b) $\frac{2}{5}$

9. 220°

MATHEMATICS GENERAL PAPER 2 2008

1. £102·55

2. 3 hours 30 minutes

3. (a) 3·575 kg

   (b) 3

4. (a)

Number of M-shapes (m)	1	2	3	4		15
Number of bars (b)	4	7	**10**	**13**		**46**

   (b) $b = 3m + 1$

   (c) 25

5. 17 cm

6. 40%

7.

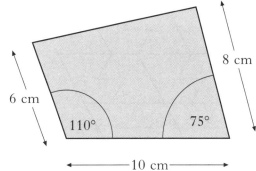

8. (a) $t = 8$

   (b) $4(5x - 3y)$

9. 7·326 m

10.

Parking time (hours)	Frequency	Parking time × frequency
1	28	28
2	22	44
3	10	30
4	15	60
5	11	55
6	5	30
7	9	63
	Total = 100	Total = 310

   Mean parking time = 3·1 hours

11. 77

12. 24·4°

13. (a) 399 000 cm³

   (b) 131·9 cm

MATHEMATICS GENERAL PAPER 1 2009 (NON-CALCULATOR)

1. (a) 2·44

   (b) 138 000

   (c) 36·7

   (d) 43·2

2. $2·96 \times 10^{-2}$

3. (a)

Number of sections (s)	1	2	3	4	5		11
Number of metal rings (r)	4	9	**14**	**19**	**24**		**54**

   (b) $r = 5s - 1$

   (c) 16

4.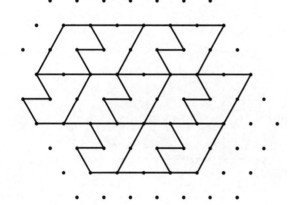

5. (a), (b), (c)

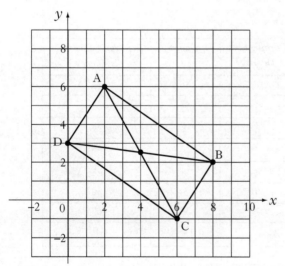

6. $-17°C$

7. 200 grams

8. (a)

5	3	3	4	6	8
6	1	2	3	5	7	8
7	0	4	6	6
8	3	4	5	8

   n = 19   5|3 = 5·3

   (b) 6·7 cm

9. 143°

MATHEMATICS GENERAL PAPER 2 2009

1. 42 mph

2. £56·80

3. 641 cm²

4. (a) 2h 15 min

   (b) 2255

5. (a) $3(2c - 5d)$

   (b) $a + 15$

6. (a)

Selections				Cost
Drama	Sport	Movies	Music	52
Drama	Sport	Movies	Kids	54
Drama	Sport	Kids	Music	49
Drama	Movies	Kids	Music	44
Sport	Movies	Kids	Music	57

   (b) Sport, Movies, Kids, Music (£57)

7. 3·3 hrs

8. 3·4 m

9. £22·25

10. £74·40

11. 8·45

12. Yes, 3m³ left over

13.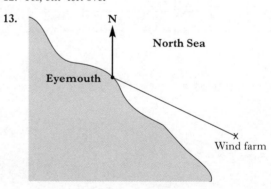

14. 5 cm

MATHEMATICS GENERAL PAPER 1 2010 (NON-CALCULATOR)

1. (a) 7·99

   (b) 300·8

   (c) 6·7

   (d) $16\frac{1}{3}$

2. $5\cdot8 \times 10^9$

3. 23°C

4.

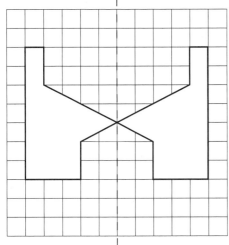

5.
```
1 | 1 2 3 4 4 5 5 6 7 7
2 | 1 6 7
3 | 1 2 3
4 | 2 4 6
5 | 1
```

6. (a)

Number of alphabet tiles (a)	1	2	3	4	5		12
Number of coloured tiles (c)	6	10	14	18	22		50

   (b) $c = 4a + 2$

   (c) 21

7. £50

8. 20%

9. 1 = 20   b = 16

10. 21°

MATHEMATICS GENERAL PAPER 2 2010

1. (a) 112

   (b) 255

2. £1280

3.

Apples	Oranges	Grapes	Pears	Melon	Cost
✓	✓		✓		£4·01
✓	✓	✓			£4·94
✓	✓			✓	£4·43
✓			✓	✓	£4·79
	✓		✓	✓	£4·74

4. (a) $-5, -1, 3$

   (b)

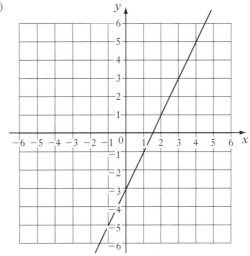

5. Yes, speed only 15 mph

6. (a) $13c - 14$

   (b) $x = 3$

7. £125

8. 400

9. 70 m

10. 30·1°

11. (a) 82·5 km

   (b) 330 (± 2)°

12. 26·8 cm

13. 109900 cm³

14. £10·20

MATHEMATICS GENERAL PAPER 1 2011 (NON-CALCULATOR)

1. (a) 341·89

   (b) 12880

   (c) 0·043

   (d) 16

2. 2.54×10^{-3}

3. (a)

1	2	3	4		10
6	10	14	18		42

   (b) $g = 4s + 2$

   (c) 16

4. (a) 10

   (b) 26

   (c) 42

5. 72 cm²

6. −14°C

7. 95°

8. £8

9. 12·5 cm

MATHEMATICS GENERAL PAPER 2 2011

1. £810

2. (a) 4/10 or equivalent

   (b) 10/13 or equivalent

3. £20·11

4.

8 points	5 points	2 points	Total
2	0	1	18
3	0	0	24
2	1	0	21
1	2	0	18
1	1	1	15
0	3	0	15

5. (a) 225°

   (b) Southeast

6. (a) $6(3 + 2t)$

   (b) $m = 10$

7. No, only 10·4 hours available and 11 hours required

8.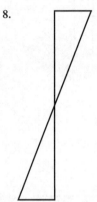

9. 75·96

10. 2 hours 25 minutes

11. (a)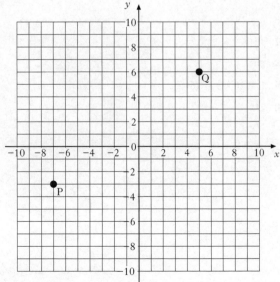

   (b) 9/12

12. 54·8 cm

13. 71·6

14. 16 (complete metres)

MATHEMATICS GENERAL PAPER 1 2012 (NON-CALCULATOR)

1. (a) 16·69

   (b) 219·6

   (c) 12·8

   (d) $\frac{7}{12}$

2. (£) $2\cdot72 \times 10^7$

3. (a)

1	2	3	4	5		12
6	11	**16**	**21**	**26**		**61**

   (b) $c = 5s + 1$

   (c) 23

4. (a) 42, 56

   (b) 43

   (c) 50

5. 122 (°)

6. 0·05 $\frac{1}{5}$ $\frac{5}{10}$ 0·505   51%

7. (£)120(·00)

8. 900

9. 23 26

10. 161(°)

MATHEMATICS GENERAL PAPER 2 2012

1. 9·6 (km/h)

2. Diagram completed

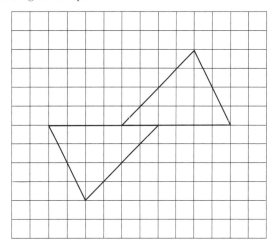

3. (£)455

4. 233(°)

5. (£)264·50

6. (a) $-3, 1, 5$

   (b) Line plotted

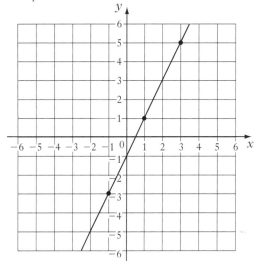

7. 126(·5) (cm)

8. (£)95

9. (a) $x = 5$

   (b) $3(4t + 3u)$

10. Yes, the mean time of the 2nd semi-final was 0·01s less than the 1st

11. Correct bar chart drawn

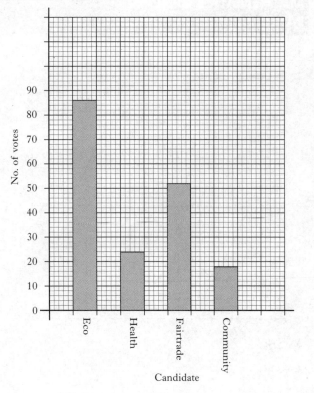

12. 7 (cm)

13. 25·6 (m)

14. 7·97 (cm)

Hey! I've done it